Guitar Player

Presents

CARLOS
SANTANA

GuitarPlayer
Presents

CARLOS SANTANA

Edited by Michael Molenda

Backbeat Books

An Imprint of Hal Leonard Corporation
New York

Portions of this book are adapted from articles that originally appeared in *Guitar Player* magazine, 1970–2008.

Published in cooperation with Music Player Network, New Bay Media, LLC, and *Guitar Player* magazine. *Guitar Player* magazine is a registered trademark of New Bay Media, LLC.

Published in 2010 by Backbeat Books
An Imprint of Hal Leonard Corporation
7777 West Bluemound Road
Milwaukee, WI 53213

Trade Book Division Editorial Offices
19 West 21st Street, New York, NY 10010

Printed in the United States of America

Book design by Damien Castaneda

Library of Congress Cataloging-in-Publication Data is available upon request.

ISBN 978-0-87930-976-3

www.backbeatbooks.com

CONTENTS

PREFACE

· ·

The commercial music business can be a cesspool of vicious ambition, broken dreams, dashed hopes, rampant unfaithfulness, and outright dishonesty. It can destroy hearts and minds, and it can toss fragile artists into an emotional morass so far removed from a Norman Rockwell view of life that many never recover. Drugs. Alcohol. Divorce. Death. Isolation. Rehab. You've read all the sordid stories, and witnessed the destruction on reality television and episodes of VH1's *Behind the Music*. Dante's *Inferno* has nothing on the music biz.

And yet, through four decades of cultural tumult and renewal—in a career that spans from Woodstock to Warped Tours, Vietnam to Iraq, Reaganomics to the treachery of Bernie Madoff, print media to Twitter, and beyond—Carlos Santana has wielded his guitar like a lightsaber of bliss. Every note he frees from his strings is bathed in joy, spirituality, and passion, and he plays for *you*. He avoids ego, embraces the Divine, and allows his heart, rather than his head, to direct his fingers, his tone, and his soaring melodicism. He is also an exuberant seeker of knowledge who finds beauty in all music, from Miles Davis and John Coltrane, to the Beatles and the Beach Boys, to Green Day and Mastodon.

This cheerful open-mindedness has not been without risk. Some people have viewed Santana's spiritualism, his sojourn as a disciple of Sri Chinmoy, and his gentle evangelical bent as too much heavenly woo-woo when all they want to hear is the man play his guitar. But Santana has always been authentic—even to the point of admitting that Frank Zappa may have addressed the phrase "Shut Up and Play Your Guitar" to him—and he has never shied away from expressing who he is as a musician and as a planetary citizen. This is a very successful and reasonably contented man who has also fallen, failed, and faced despair, and those experiences remain a part of his every bend, trill, lick, riff, and melodic run. In this way, Santana is as much a bluesman as a pop star, although—to use his own words—he "paints with a different brush."

In this book, you'll absorb many of the elements that make Carlos Santana a legendary guitarist—well, at least the bits that can be set down on ink and paper. Through his many *Guitar Player* interviews, you'll get exhaustive insights into what drives his creativity, where he derives the foundation of his musicality, what tools he uses to get his transcendent tone, and much more. The *Guitar Player* lessons—crafted by master transcriptionists Jesse Gress and Andy Ellis—reveal explicit "physical" keys to Santana's melodic and harmonic approaches.

Santana has been a longtime friend of *Guitar Player*. On many occasions, he has publicly stated that it's one of his favorite publications. The magazine itself has often been blessed with incredible writers who hold vast knowledge and enthusiasm for guitarcraft, and this volume collects unabridged Santana interviews from 1970 to 2008 by some of the best: Fred Stuckey, Michael Brooks, Dan Forte, Jas Obrecht, James Rotondi, Andy Ellis, Jesse Gress, Darrin Fox, and Gary Brawer.

As you'll (hopefully) see, the intense collaboration between a magnificent artist who trusts his interviewers, and talented authors who voraciously dig into the mysteries of tone, technique, and creativity delivers an extraordinary degree of depth and musical intimacy. It's like standing behind a magician and seeing the architecture of magic. Enjoy!

Michael Molenda
Editor in Chief, *Guitar Player*

Many thanks to all the writers and editors who have made Guitar Player *the preeminent publication for obsessed guitarists since 1967. I also want to salute my mom, my family, my friends, and Cheryl Doll—all of whom help "keep the music in me" (apologies to Kiki Dee).*

INTERVIEWS

1.

"MUSIC IS LOPSIDED IF YOU JUST PLAY FOR YOURSELF"

· ·

by Fred Stuckey, June 1970

One phenomenon of contemporary music is the incredible speed with which rock groups can climb out of obscurity and into multimillion-dollar success stories. The best example I can think of is the recent emergence of a San Francisco band bearing the last name of a guitar player bred in the backstreets of Tijuana, a tawdry border town between California and Mexico.

Santana's first album, surprisingly entitled *Santana*, has sold somewhere in excess of a million copies and is still selling. How many musicians can claim a platinum record for their first effort? Not many.

Unlike most rock bands, Santana's hit tune "Evil Ways" is being played on both AM and FM radio, on both Top-40 and underground radio. Santana has caught the attention of the "bubble gum," commercial rock audiences as well as the sophisticates of rock among underground audiences. The musical qualities unique to Santana are elusive and not easily identifiable. But the band has something that most everybody can get into.

Getting to Carlos Santana, the band's leader and lead-guitar player, was a hassle. I had to wind through a maze of promoters, booking agents, managers, secretaries, and friends. I finally talked with Carlos at the band's rehearsal studio in the exclusive Pacific Heights district of San Francisco. The location of the studio in that high-rent neighborhood didn't fit with my preconception of the band's character. I remembered Santana as the group of brown, black, and white street musicians playing to Fillmore West audiences with the exuberance and abandon of America's hip youth. After the difficulty of getting to the band, I was expecting arrogant and jiving rock "stars."

Carlos Santana is well-spoken and hospitable. He is preoccupied with the band's music, and would rather play it than talk about it. Like most rock musicians, he approaches music from an emotional rather than an academic level. He said: "The most spectacular things I play are when I'm not programmed to play a certain thing, but when I'm free to play what I feel."

At 22, Carlos is successful, but he doesn't think much about it. He has no pretentions about being the most polished and professional of guitar players. But he is serious about what he does, and he plays hard. On stage, he writhes and grimaces to the music, hunching his shoulders and rolling his head from side to side. As he nods back and forth, his long, bushy black hair fans the air.

Carlos recently switched to a 1962 Gibson SG guitar. About the guitar and strings he said in slightly broken English: "I take my guitar to this cat who treats guitars just like you treat a woman. He uses an instrument that takes measurements in millimeters to adjust the strings the way I like it. I like my strings to lie up from the fretboard—you know, not too close. A little while ago, I switched to Ernie Ball Super Slinky strings. I found out that with those strings you can bend notes without breaking your fingers. On my other guitar, I use Gretsch strings. They're harder, and they produce more bass."

Rhythm is the cornerstone of Santana's sound. Incorporating Latin and Afro percussion instruments into the overall sound, Carlos added Mike Carabello on congas, Jose Chepito Areas on Timbales, and Mike Shrieve on drums. Powerful and complex rhythms frame the solos of Carlos on guitar and Gregg Rolie on organ. Dave Brown carries the bass lines.

I asked Carlos about his Mexican origins and Santana's heavy reliance on rhythm. "When I was a kid I listened to Latin music, but I really wasn't all that turned on by it. I dug more rock and roll and blues—you know, Chicago blues. Latin music, if you know how to control it and keep from overstating it—and can keep from letting it get boring—can make rock music very exciting. It's a part of what we play. In our music there's a lot of Latin and Afro rhythms going on. Some rhythms, like 6/8 time, we use to lead us into Afro rhythms. The timbales and conga players put down those rhythms as the bottom of the sound."

Listening to the tempo, Carlos bends and punches his guitar notes to complement the time scheme, and to build the music into crescendos and climaxes. He lends continuity to the rising and falling quality of Santana's tunes by repeating riffs at strategic points. Good examples of the way Carlos uses note patterns to signal breaks in the rhythm are the tracks "Waiting" and "Jingo" on the *Santana* album.

"The most spectacular things I play are when I'm not programmed to play a certain thing, but when I'm free to play what I feel."

Carlos talked about his picking technique. "The way I pick depends on what chops I'm doing in any particular song. On some chops, you can play like an acoustic guitar with the palm of your hand resting on the bridge. On some funky things, you can't rest your hand on anything—particularly on rhythm or chord things. I use a triangular, elastic nylon pick. They don't bend, and they'll last you forever if you don't lose them."

At key points, Carlos holds single notes through chord changes and shifts in tempo. He gets a sustaining, distorted sound out of his guitar. He said: "It feels really good to hold a note for days, to control the feedback on just one beam of power. Sometimes, the way you can hold a note depends on how you set the Tone and Volume controls on the guitar and amp—I use Fender amplifiers—and that depends on the size of the hall. To get a sustained or distorted sound, I don't necessarily use a fuzz tone. I can get that same sound with a broken speaker in an amp, and it sounds better."

Basing his solo riffs around the blues scale, Carlos owes his early influences to American music.

"I first started playing the old Top-40 stuff—the old rhythm and blues tunes like 'Blue Moon.' Then I got into B. B. King. I used to play on Revolution Street in Tijuana. Some of the brothers used to come down from San Diego, and we would play blues stuff in small clubs down there.

"In Mexico, I played the violin for six years. I worked through some heavy music books with songs like 'Poet and Peasant' in them—really intricate classical stuff. Playing the violin taught me how to hold notes when somebody else is playing, when to play and when not to play—what to play and what not to play. Right now, I want to learn more about music so I can contribute more of me to it."

Carlos was part of the early San Francisco underground rock scene. He guested as lead guitarist on a blues track on the *Adventures* album recorded live at the Fillmore West by Mike Bloomfield and Al Kooper. We talked about the fading distinction between commercial and underground rock. I asked Carlos how he felt about having a Top-40 hit.

"You know, I met the other guys in the band on the streets in San Francisco. We were just jamming around. In those days, we were playing what a lot of people are playing now—hard rock and blues and Cream-style things. About Top-40 stuff, I want to give and take with music. If I just play for myself and people don't relate to me, then I'm not saying what I want to say. Music is lopsided if you just play for yourself. You've got to play what people want to hear, too."

No question that Santana plays what rock audiences want to hear.

Still preoccupied with the day's rehearsing and staring off across the room, Carlos told me how Santana comes up with material.

"When we put together a tune, somebody comes in with an idea, and we all work on it. We don't play from charts. All of us contribute to putting a song together, and somehow we feel closer that way. When everybody can play the notes and feelings that are his, then everybody feels happier about them when we play them onstage. The notes and feelings have to be your own. The chops you play that you have created come across as being warmer than the notes that somebody tells you to play. Like on a song, when I feel that the whole thing is solid, and the rhythm is there, and everyone is relating to everyone else, then I can take off. When I solo, I do the most spectacular things when I'm not thinking about what I'm playing. When I'm feeling it is when it's good. For any musician the moments of gold are when you just sit back and think, 'Wow, how did I do that?'"

For an album recorded and mixed in the studio, *Santana* is not without flaws, particularly in regard to balance. On the "Savor" track, the organ solo is buried by the percussion instruments, and on the "Persuasion" track, the vocal could be louder. At times, the length of instrumental breaks stretches to the thin point of the soloing capabilities of the musicians. But, all in all, *Santana* is an exciting album.

As we were talking, Carlos plugged in his SG and started to play a slow tempo, *C*-minor blues. I sat down at the organ, and the organist sat down at the drums. The rest of Santana drifted into the studio one at a time and picked up their instruments. Moments later, Carlos was swaying back and forth, his eyes squinted closed and shoulders hunched. He traded 12-bar solos with us, one for one, until it was time to get back to business.

2.

"I AM THE STRING, AND THE SUPREME IS THE MUSICIAN"

by Michael Brooks, November 1974

In the aftermath of his highly successful union with Mahavishnu John McLaughlin on Columbia's *Love Devotion Surrender*, Carlos Santana, lead guitarist with the group Santana, is still in an evolutionary process. In 1973, he performed 312 concerts, and recently finished an album with Alice Coltrane [at press time, tentatively titled *Illuminations*], feeling he was "compelled to do it by the Supreme."

Yes, Carlos is still deeply involved with his, and John McLaughlin's, guru, Sri Chinmoy. He is also producing music with "high spiritual content," and foresees no change from his present path.

The following interview with Carlos Santana was an effort to gain a better understanding of how his guitar and guitar playing blends or contrasts with his spiritual life.

Now that you have given yourself to the Supreme, do you find your music at a higher improvisational level?

Sometimes—especially when I truly humble myself. But, a lot of times, what I hear, and what the Supreme hears are two different things. Sometimes, when I listen to musical passages which come out of me—when I open my eyes—I find that I am concentrating too much on the music, and it makes it sound without feeling. Sometimes, I find myself still living in the illusion that I've got to do it the way I hear it. But when I do that, it doesn't come out right—it sounds too thought out. You know, you can tell when somebody makes a speech from his heart—it's just spontaneous—and you can tell when someone has been studying up, just through his words and tone. The most natural thing on earth is your heart—your soul—because it rarely goes out of tune with God. What goes out of tune is your mind and your body.

How do you relate your spiritual life to your guitar?

I am the string, and the Supreme is the musician.

But when you have humbled yourself to the Supreme, and he is playing through you, do you ever find a point where the Supreme's music is just not happening?

Sometimes, but when that happens, it's because my mind is still in the way. I said before that I'm the string, and that's all I am, because I go out of tune just like a string goes out of tune. By that I mean that I am not totally consistent yet. I've got a long way to go before I can be in any kind of environment and still keep that oneness with the Supreme, so I don't start swearing and trying to be stupidly proud. But when I'm really in tune with the Supreme, my guru, and my instrument, forget it, man, because it's totally beyond anything—and that's where I want to be. I just want to be in service to the Supreme. It's getting to where I don't even expect to understand a song until after I've played it and heard it back. I hear a sound and I go for it, but I know that if I hear exactly how it sounds while I'm playing it, it's not going to be that good, because then my mind is controlling it. It's like sometimes I'm not aware I can do some of these things on my guitar, because, in reality, I'm not doing them, they are being done through me—which is one of the highest places anyone can reach.

Many of our readers want to know what equipment you used on *Caravanserai*?

I used a new 1971 Gibson Les Paul with a cherry sunburst finish and a beefed-up Fender Twin Reverb for most of it. For strings, I used a mixed set with the trebles of .009, .011, and .015 from a Gibson Lights set. Then, for the bass strings, I used Ernie Ball strings, gauged .024, .036, and .042.

Do you change strings frequently?

At least every two concerts. If the concerts are long, then I change after each show. For studio work, I like to put new ones on just about every other day. Usually, I can tell by just looking at them if they need changing, because the color is different, and that's when they begin to slip and become harder to tune.

Have you switched instruments since the album with John?

II

"I AM THE STRING, AND THE SUPREME IS THE MUSICIAN"

Oh, I just flipped over this Gibson L6-S. It's not like I'm endorsing it, but that axe is beautiful. It's got more accessible frets, and the pickups are just incredible. With the controls, I can make it sound like a Stratocaster, a Telecaster, an SG, or a Les Paul. I get them all. It has a very fast fingerboard, and it's clean sounding.

Have you used the Gibson L6-S in the studio yet?

Yeah, I used it on the album I recently did with Alice Coltrane.

What are you presently using for an amp?

It's called a Mesa/Boogie amplifier. I'm going to turn Mahavishnu onto it, and it'll just flip him right out. There's nothing like it on the market. It gives you three volume controls. The first one on the left I crank up to 7, and then I put the Master Volume control on half, and I can play like in a hotel, but it's screaming. But if I want to play at a place like the Berkeley Community Theatre or a bigger hall, I just turn the master up to 5, and I can project. If I want to play Winterland or someplace bigger, I just turn it up to 7.

You have gained a notable reputation for your sustain. Have you ever used sustain devices of any sort?

I never use sustain devices at all. I just do it the old-fashioned way—get close to the amplifier.

Do you have to search out the optimum position of your guitar and amp for each sound setup, or do you have it pretty much down now?

Well, I still have to move back and forth until I can find just the right kind of sustain. Sometimes, I hear all these other overtones coming in, maybe out of tune, you know. So I have to keep moving around until I get it, because I don't know how to use those gadgets and stuff like that. I mean, I know there are products in the stores which you can use to get good sustain, but they all sound over-electrified to me. I like the pure sustain without speakers cracking and without overloading the amp.

As far as your guitar setting for sustain, do you find it better with full-on bass?

Well, for me, I use full midrange. Like, I don't know exactly what I do for sustain, and it has taken me some time to get it, but I hear the sound in my head, and I know what it sounds like, and I go for it. You just have to keep moving around and experiment with different settings, because each instrument is a little different, and so is each amp.

To what do you specifically attribute your fine sustain?

Carlos Santana rocking a Les Paul during a 1970s-era concert. (PHOTOFEST)

"I AM THE STRING, AND THE SUPREME IS THE MUSICIAN"

It's all in the pickups, man, the super-hum-bucking pickups. The sustain you get from those you wouldn't believe.

"My thing is to try to open hearts and minds to observe a deeper awareness— to real music, to divine music, to a real purpose in life."

Were you satisfied with the outcome of *Love Devotion Surrender*?

Well, personally I think it would be a waste of time to do another album, just because I didn't think it was truly happening 100 percent on that record, you know, with the people playing. If we do another, I want to be more part of the rest of the people. Last time, John chose half, and I chose half, and like it wasn't happening after a while. We weren't really playing together. At times it was, but we really had to struggle to get it together. No matter who I'm playing with, I like to feel it's more than a gig. It's like John says, "It's a mission, a divine mission," and that's how I like to treat concerts. Like, anyone can make money, man. I could be a dishwasher if I wanted to make money, but my thing is to try to open hearts and minds to observe a deeper awareness—to real music, to divine music, to a real purpose in life. By this way, I can better myself, and we're all trying to do that.

In your guitar playing, how does the technical element relate to the spiritual element?

They both have to go hand-in-hand. It's like going back to Leonardo da Vinci. For him to reflect all his artwork, he had to get his chops out before he could try to reflect all that perfection the Supreme gave him. On the album with Mahavishnu, all our spirituality, in order to manifest itself, had to come out as high and as deep as da Vinci, but we rehearsed maybe a month at the most. But, really, it's all in the conviction that you do it with. It's like all those people calling Mahavishnu's and my album "far-out" and "outer-space," but to me it is like an offering of flowers to God. It is the Supreme, your highest self. But I know this music has nothing to do with "far-out" or "outer-space." You see, when you humble yourself to the Supreme, you wake up in the morning, and what happens is that I am the instrument, and the guitar is just the guitar. I just don't wear the pin, and say I'm into spirituality. I live the part, and I've *got* to live the part, because anybody can tell when it's not sincere. And the same goes for music. If you don't have the conviction, or if you aren't feeling your music, you can tell, and I can tell. That's why I really laugh when I see all these albums sold like "King of the Guitar." There's only one king, man, and that's the Supreme. And when he plays through you, according to your capacity, it's like music from beyond, and that's what I'm hungry for.

Do you find yourself playing a lot more, now that you have given yourself to the Supreme? Playing not only with a totally different perspective, but also playing more in hours per day?

Yeah. Like if I'm not practicing my guitar and my technique, I'm reading certain types of books which make me constantly aware of how much conviction, surrender, devotion I have to have so that I don't go out of tune. So when I play, all those doubts and wrong notes don't come into the picture, because really there's no such thing as wrong notes, you know. I'm finding that because my ears are so trained to play in a certain vein, I'm having to break out of certain playing habits. It's like when you're a kid, and you have a car, and people tell you a car won't go up a wall, it should just stay on the road. But that's a bunch of baloney. On the technical side, I thoroughly agree with the advice, otherwise you could kill yourself. But when you're a kid, and you just get a car, you start taking all those chances. That's the same with music, man. It's like Miles Davis taking all those chances and ending up by training a lot of people to hear different things—like all those chords Miles was doing with his band. You can hear them on commercials now. So kids are getting educated, and people are growing, but they don't even know at what rate they are growing.

When did you grow into the awareness of that jazz/Indian-flavored music as being your highest point. Was it through Mahavishnu?

Right. He brought some cassettes over the first time he came to my house. At that time, Indian music was like an ocean too big to cross. Like when you're a kid, and somebody puts you on to symphony music, and it just turns you right off. It's too deep. Some music just goes right over you, and you start yawning. And it was sort of like that, you know. John Coltrane's music used to do that to me. It's so heavy, it's like eating a big meal. But, after a while, I got hungry for it. You see, I was going to all these clubs and getting tired of hearing all this mediocrity. People just playing for the money, and not playing it because they were living it, or being it. But now, I'm really hungry, and I guess my ears expect a lot more—no matter what kind of music it is. I really expect that sincerity—that conviction. Between John, and now Indian music, I can sincerely say that they're molding me to be what I have been trying to be for a long time. It's like "they're molding me" is a way to say it, but really what I mean is that my spiritual master, guru Sri Chinmoy, John, and Alice Coltrane are all taking me home, man. They're taking me home to the place I've been away from for so long— and home is one with God. I can totally be myself, and not what my mind wants me to be or what the system wants me to be, because they are different things. What God wants me to be is it for me. And I can't delay because everything else is just an illusion. And I can tell in the music if it's being played from the heart. Then—and only then—is it coming from God.

When you find this perfection—or get very close to this perfection—do you feel it's your obligation to spread it?

Sure. That's why it takes sheer conviction to do what I'm doing. Like my parents, friends, and some other people expect me to portray the role of yesterday. Like some tell me, "Man, I really liked the way you used to play all your songs." And I say, "Well, why don't you go to all those clubs where they are playing music like I used to do." You know, I've got to move on. And I'm not moving on to impress anybody—that's not the thing for me. For me, it's just like the more I can be of service to humanity. Like in a concert—if I can inspire one more brother or sister to start getting himself together as far as praying or meditating or just humbling himself to the Supreme, then I'm making far more progress than anybody else. Because that person's energy will be conducted to the right channel—to the right time and place. And we can end this disillusionment, this frustration, this destruction, and all this ignorance.

Do you feel your spiritual path will always be involved with the guitar and music?

For right now, it all seems to be music. I have a tremendous amount of freedom still. We all do. I don't have the freedom that I used to have, though, because then I didn't have as much awareness. By that I mean that if you are not aware, like of a strong conviction, or even the universal laws—the Ten Commandments—and they haven't hit you as something to obey, then you can do anything you want. But once they start touching you, once they have soaked into your heart, you can't get away with it as much, because the Supreme is right there making it all come back.

3.

"IT TOOK ME A WHILE TO REALIZE THAT YOUR INDIVIDUALITY IS A VERY BEAUTIFUL GIFT"

by Dan Forte, June 1978

Tenor saxophonist John Coltrane, one of modern jazz's true innovators, once said, "We are always searching. I think that now we are at the point of finding." Devadip Carlos Santana, like Coltrane, is a searcher—or, as he puts it, a seeker. The similarities between the two artists don't stop there. As with Coltrane's music, Santana's music has reflected the spiritual lifestyle he has chosen. Like Coltrane, he is an innovator, and, above all, an individual voice on his instrument, the guitar.

John Coltrane was a major inspiration for Carlos, so the parallels are no doubt more than coincidence. The title tune of the Santana band's seventh album, *Welcome*, was a Coltrane composition. The guitarist collaborated with the saxophonist's widow, pianist/harpist Turiya Alice Coltrane, on the album *Illuminations*. At one stage, Devadip would even sleep with a tape of Coltrane music playing all night long.

But Santana was wise enough to know that there could only be one John Coltrane, and he listened to the music for inspiration—not to cop lines or even stylistic modes. Carlos Santana is such an individualist that it's difficult to hear direct traces of the musicians he cites as influences, except on rare occasions. He will talk for hours about his deep love for the blues, rattling off an endless list of favorite performers of the genre. Yet in his ten albums with the Santana band and his various solo projects, he has never recorded a blues tune—at least not in standard blues form. The blues, like the other factors that make up Santana's sound, is reflected as a feeling—not as notes or rhythms.

To this day, the name Santana brings to mind a picture of a battery of Latin percussionists behind their leader, who leans backwards, eyes clenched shut in concentration, as he squeezes the notes from his guitar. The Santana band was the first group to successfully blend Latin and Afro rhythms with rock music. Originally known as the Santana Blues Band—later shortened to its leader's surname—the group built a strong following at Bill Graham's Fillmore Auditorium in San Francisco, eventually headlining shows with the likes of Taj Mahal, the Youngbloods, and Melanie before they had even recorded. The young band received national acclaim thanks to the Woodstock festival in 1969, the same year their first LP, *Santana*, debuted. *Santana* produced two hit singles in "Jingo" and "Evil Ways," and turned platinum within a year—an achievement few groups of that period could claim.

More hit albums and singles followed—"Oye Como Va," "Black Magic Woman/Gypsy Queen," "No One To Depend On"—despite numerous personnel changes in the group. The Santana band's direction changed as did its guitarist/leader's ideals. Guitarist Neal Schon and singer/keyboardist Gregg Rolie left to form Journey following the group's first major departure from Latin rock, *Caravanserai*. The album, the band's fourth, revealed the jazzier influences that had been absorbing much of Carlos Santana's energies. Artists such as Coltrane, Charles Lloyd, McCoy Tyner, Thelonious Monk, Miles Davis (whom Santana calls "the Muhammad Ali of music"), and the group Weather Report provided the inspiration that had previously come from B. B. King, Jimmy Reed, and others.

What Carlos was searching for, musically and personally, he found in Sri Chinmoy, his spiritual guru. Santana was introduced to Sri Chinmoy by electrifying guitarist Mahavishnu John McLaughlin. The two artists joined forces on *Love Devotion Surrender* in 1973, which was as much a religious statement as it was a musical one. Though McLaughlin has since dropped the Mahavishnu title and is no longer a follower of the guru, Devadip (Santana's spiritual name) has stuck close to Chinmoy's teachings.

"IT TOOK ME A WHILE TO REALIZE THAT YOUR INDIVIDUALITY IS A VERY BEAUTIFUL GIFT"

But the more Santana's music began to mirror the tranquility and inner peace Devadip had found, the less it sounded like the energetic, feverish group that had insured "street music's" inclusion in the list of psychedelic San Francisco rock outfits. Carlos began to realize that the concert-opening moments of silent meditation—and the extended improvisational excursions—were alienating some of his old fans. People wanted to move and dance.

While on tour with McLaughlin in 1973, Santana dropped by a Seattle beer bar to jam with one of his early, pre-guru inspirations, Elvin Bishop. The ex-Butterfield Blues Band guitarist's brand of ham-and-eggs rock and blues—and the crowd's involvement with it—brought Carlos to the realization that "the highest form of spirituality is joy. If you don't have that, man, then I don't care for spirituality."

Along with the two longest-surviving members of the Santana band—keyboardist Tom Coster and percussionist Ndugu Leon Chancler—Devadip took a retrospective look at the group's history, and sought to reignite the spark that had separated Santana from other rock bands in the first place. The result of their research appeared in the 1976 LP *Amigos*, and articles immediately proclaimed the "return" of Santana. The year 1977 produced two more albums on basically the same track—*Festival* and the double-album *Moonflower*—and Santana's international popularity is now probably as high as ever.

Along with the increased recognition of the band, Carlos Santana's guitar skills have finally received the notice they deserve, and his position in the elite of rock guitarists is secure to say the least. Last year's *Moonflower* was voted Best Record of the Year in the first annual Bay Area Music Awards, sponsored by San Francisco's *BAM* magazine, and, in the same poll, readers chose Carlos Best Guitarist. In last year's *Guitar Player* Readers' Poll, he placed high in both the Rock and Overall categories.

Whether or not one chooses to use adjectives such as "best" when describing Carlos' abilities on guitar, the 30-year-old instrumentalist must surely rate as one of the most distinctive and emotional players around today, regardless of style. And whether or not one wishes to believe in the spiritual path Devadip has chosen to follow, one thing is obvious—it works for him. And Santana and his music will no doubt survive long after other artists are either dried up or burned out.

When you were growing up, did your father play in mariachi bands? Did he teach you things?

Yes. I started playing the violin first. I was playing Beethoven's "Minuet in *G*" and "Poet and Peasant Overture" by Von Suppé—you know, classical songs. But I hated the violin. I just hated the sound of it, and the smell of it. And, to me, anything I played on the violin sounded like Jack Benny when he was fooling around [*laughs*]. I know he could really play well, but when he was joking around, that's what I sounded like at my best. I couldn't get into it. Later, I saw this band in Tijuana, where I grew up, and they were totally imitating B. B. King, Ray Charles, Bobby Bland, and Little Richard. They were from Tijuana, and when I heard them playing, I said, "Oh, man! This is the stuff I want to get into." I was about 11 or so, and it was the first blues I'd heard. And then Javier Batiz, the guitar player, took me to his house, and we got to be friends. He had a very beautiful sound, and you could tell that he lived with records by B. B. King, Ray Charles, and Little Richard. That's what knocked me out. I'd see my sister screaming over Elvis Presley, and even though I was a kid, I had the attitude that it was just a fad. But I never felt empathy with Mexican music. Not that I hated it—I just couldn't relate to it. I usually equated Mexican music with drunk Mexicans having a brawl, and overemphasizing the macho trips, so I really couldn't get into it. I grew up with that environment. I could get into the blues more. It was more natural to me.

When you moved to San Francisco, did you eventually get into the white blues movement that was happening at that time?

Paul Butterfield? Yeah, he was the one who started the whole thing for a lot of people. See, when I came to America, my American friends would be listening to the Dave Clark Five and the Beach Boys, and I couldn't stand that. I'd say, "Why are you into these guys? They aren't even saying nothing, man. Listen to Ray Charles and Bobby Bland." And they'd say, "That stuff is old." And all of a sudden, two things hit me: One was seeing Paul Butterfield and Muddy Waters, and the other was Cream's first record [*Fresh Cream*]. It just totally turned me around. I said, "How can these guys play blues like that?" That's when I started to play hooky from Mission High and started hanging out on Mission Street. Stan Marcum, who subsequently became my first manager, took me to Winterland to see Paul Butterfield and Muddy Waters when Muddy had Little Walter on harp. Man, I was knocked out for weeks. I was in a daze. I don't know how many dishes I broke working as a dishwasher after that. I couldn't believe what blues could do to people. See, I wasn't getting loaded at the time, so when I went to Winterland, I was totally aware of my surroundings. It wasn't like when people get loaded and become so overly aware that they [*whistles*]—they're everywhere at the same time, so they miss something. But I could see people's eyes and faces and the way they were reacting when the band was playing the blues. I could see that the group was feeding these people, and they were feeding me. It was one of the most fantastic concerts I've ever been to.

Did that lead you to search out records by older bluesmen?

Yeah, yeah. I got into Little Milton and all those people. I think the blues is about the most beautiful contribution that the black man has given to the United States, because anybody can claim them. If you're in high school, you can feel the blues, because most people who are in high school don't know where to go. You ask them, "What do you want to be when you grow up?" "I don't know." And that in itself is a burden, and that can give you a certain amount of the downers, you know, the blues. So when you listen to James Cotton or Little Walter or Junior Wells, you totally feel like they know, and they've been through what you're going through. Being from the West, that's the most universal music. Maybe if you're from India, you can't relate to it, but being from the West, that's the most universal music we have.

Did the original Santana Blues Band play blues standards?

We did songs by B. B. King, Ray Charles—like "Woke Up This Morning" and "Mary Ann"—and we would do our own versions of the first two Butterfield albums. We even did "East-West." And that's when I eventually started getting into drugs. I always saw so many people around me taking drugs, but the only thing I remember that would stop me from trying it was that I would practice with the band for a long time to get some numbers down pat, and we'd really be burning. Then we'd take a break, and they'd all go smoke some weed, come back, and forget the changes. Because weed can make you trip up, you know. And I hated that. I said, "Man, that's not the way we rehearsed it." But, once, somebody left the house and left a joint in the ashtray for me, and I had *Sergeant Pepper* or *Revolver* by the Beatles on the turntable. So I thought I'd see what it was about. It does make you aware of other things, other possibilities. But it's like tennis shoes. If you wear size eight, why put on size six? You already went through that three years ago, and it doesn't fit anymore. That's how I feel about drugs now—they just don't fit me. But if I hadn't ever taken drugs I'd probably be kind of square and more prejudiced. I don't think I would have been as open to things like [jazz flautist] Charles Lloyd and [saxophonist] John Handy. It can make you receptive and sensitive to a certain level, right? The Beatles, Cream, and the Yardbirds were all doing it, so you say, "Gee, maybe there's something to it." It did play a role. Plus, when I was a kid in Tijuana, I'd see everybody smoking pot, but I wouldn't do it.

Playing American blues music in Tijuana, did you relate more to the Mexican people or the Americans?

All the musicians that I hung around with had this beautiful pride in being hip to all the black musicians who'd come down from America to cop drugs. They'd come down to this club where I worked, and that's how I became aware of that music. They were singing the latest songs by Ray Charles and Bobby Bland, and we'd have to learn them. So I wasn't really into a Mexican atmosphere—I was more into a black man's atmosphere. Like I said, it took me a while to relate to the Beach Boys and the Beatles because of that. So I don't think I relate as much to Mexican music and Mexican people as I do to the low-income Americans. A lot of white people played over there, too, and when they played the blues you could tell that they were greatly influenced by Jerry Lee Lewis.

How old were you when you came to San Francisco?

It was 1962, so I must have been 12 or 13. It was a drag, because they put me back into junior high, because I couldn't speak English. I had to learn to adapt to a whole other way of thinking and being around kids, because I thought I was a man of the world—working and playing in this nightclub in Tijuana, watching ladies strip. We'd play for an hour, and then they'd strip for an hour, then we'd play. To me, I was a grown-up, so when I came here I had to live the life of a young adolescent all over again, and I couldn't relate. But, fortunately, I did find some musicians who helped me make the transition much faster.

Were you on your own, working for a living as a kid in Tijuana?

In Tijuana, I was working for a living. I wasn't going to school anymore. And when I came here, that was a burden, because I had to go back to school, and I hated school. I mean, I always knew I was going to be a musician even before they put me in junior high. So I couldn't see why I had to know algebra and that sort of trip. But what was fascinating—which many Americans take for granted—is that you meet so many friends in one day of school, with the different teachers and classes. In Mexico, you have the same kids all day.

Did you want to come to America, or were you content playing in clubs in Tijuana?

I was very content there, because I was making my own money, nobody was telling me what to do, and I didn't have to be home at any special time. I was living on my own. I'd had a falling-out with my parents, and they were up here already. When you're a kid, it's like nothing is a burden.

Did the Latin influences creep into the Santana band because of the things you'd heard as a kid, or did an outside musician bring that element to the band?

[*Long pause.*] It took me a long time, just now, to remember when the congas came in. We were exclusively a blues band at first. People ask me a lot of times how the change took place, and I think the reason was that we'd go around "hippy hill" and Aquatic Park in San Francisco, and they used to have congas and wine, and that's where we got the congas in the band. And then I heard Gabor Szabo, and his album *Spellbinder* has congas on it. Somebody brought this conga player to jam with us, and he threw us into a whole different thing. Actually, we never play "Latin music"—you know, it's a crossover. I just play whatever I hear.

Did you originally plan to add a conga player, yet continue playing blues?

Yeah. Even when we had a conga player it was still the Santana Blues Band. Later we got Chepito [Areas], and he was playing congas and timbales. Then we dropped the "Blues Band" and started to play more of a crossover. And we were listening to Miles and the Jazz Crusaders. After that, it was really interesting, because even Chicago came out with congas. Actually, Harvey Mandel was probably the first guy to put congas on a rock and roll album [*Cristo Redentor*]. I saw him and Charlie Musselwhite [as the Southside Sound System] at the Avalon one time, and they played "Cristo Redentor" and "Wade in the Water," and I was knocked out. I learned a lot from them. I really admire guys like Harvey Mandel whose sound I can identify, because it takes a lot of work. Nobody can say that you are born with it. You work for it, and carve your own individuality. In fact, if people want to find out how to develop this, a good way is to get a tape recorder, and for half an hour, turn out the lights in your house and get into a room that's kind of dark, where you don't have interruptions. Then just play with a rhythm machine. After a while, it's like a deck of cards on the table, and you can begin to see the riffs that came from this guy, the riffs that came from that guy, and then the two or three riffs that are yours. Then you start concentrating on yours, and, to me, that's how you develop your own individual sound. You play a couple of notes and say, "Gee, that sounds like Eric Clapton" or "That sounds like George Benson." But then you play two or three notes, and say, "Man, that's me." Not until a couple of years ago did I consciously start doing it that way. I'd just sit down, turn everything off, get a rhythm machine, and just play and play.

Do you find much time to practice guitar these days?

Yeah, I still do it a lot—as much as I can. Mainly with the rhythm machine. I practice so that my fingers will respond to what I feel. Sometimes, I have this incredible craving just to get a music teacher to teach me chords and fancy scales that you'd find in *The Thesaurus of Scales and Melodic Patterns*. I pick up that book once in a while and play two or three lines. Sometimes it scares me, because I start playing something really significant. Then, sometimes, I start sounding like everybody else, and I don't want to sound like that. I leave that stuff to Jerry Hahn and Larry Coryell, who are really great at what they do. I admire their craft, but I prefer simplicity. It's like eating. If you don't discriminate what you eat, you get sick—you know, indigestion. You have to know what's good for you. You are digesting it by learning it. It is stored up in your memory cells. Recently, I was playing a song by

"IT TOOK ME A WHILE TO REALIZE THAT YOUR INDIVIDUALITY IS A VERY BEAUTIFUL GIFT"

Roberta Flack with Donny Hathaway, "The Closer I Get to You." That's one way I practice—I put on a record when there's nobody home, and if it hits me, my face contorts and I start crying. I feel that if I can't cry to something that is moving, I'm not going to cry onstage. I think a lot of musicians become very callous, and, after a while, they can't feel pain. That's not what music is about. Before I found Sri Chinmoy, I used to take LSD just to feel pain, when all I had to do was look inside my heart and it's all there. I think that's what saved me from real hard drugs and that self-destructive path that a lot of musicians take.

Where did you learn chords?

From my father. He taught me the basic chords. My brother Jorge has been teaching me chords, and showing me how it takes years to unlearn what some books throw at you. He has been teaching me how you hear the chord and start building other chords around it just by hearing the notes. I didn't even know this stuff until about three days ago. Jorge came to my house and showed me. I'm going to stick around my brother, because he does know a lot about chords, and I need it. I think if I'm really lacking something it's harmony and chords. I don't think I'm lacking as far as imagination or vision are concerned.

Most of your playing is single-note lines—not many chords.

Right, but I know that sometimes when Tom [Coster] is playing a solo, he yearns for somebody to throw chords at him, so he can take it to something else. I can see his point. It's to his advantage and my advantage.

Do you prefer to do concept albums rather than just collections of songs?

Yes. That's the only thing that I always deal with. Mostly, it's like a vision. Each song is a vision, rather than a musical approach. It's like painting. I don't think of what kind of stroke I'm going to give it, I just picture it, and then I know instantly what instrument, what color, to use. It's just easier for me, because I can't read music. I don't know nothing about music. Tom helps me out with the music. I give him a feeling—I hear something—and we work together, and he'll say, "What you're talking about is a *B* diminished 7th. . . ." "Oh really?" I should get into music, and I probably will this year—chords and harmony. It would make it easier. I used to think it would get in the way, because I've seen musicians who are so technical with music that they always get caught on a technique of approaching a song the same way. They're bound to a technique, whereas a child who never practiced music can get the song any variety of ways, because he's not bound to a certain approach to music. Of course, I've heard a lot of pros and cons about music. I was always put off by a lot of snobbish musicians who can read music, but, fortunately, I met a lot of good musicians who had an open attitude about it. I once heard someone putting someone else down because he couldn't read music, and it was almost like in the movie *Never On Sunday*, where the mandolin player was feeling so down. They told him he wasn't a musician, because he couldn't read music. Then somebody told him, "Birds don't read music." So, in a way, it's an excuse, and I know that I should learn it and really make an effort to understand more about music, so I don't have to stutter as much. But I always feel I have enough spontaneity and enough vision not to be bound by, "Gee, I have to start with a $C\sharp$."

Have you ever felt hindered by your lack of formal training when you're playing with someone like Stanley Clarke or Chick Corea?

We can play together easily. As soon as I close my eyes, it's like where you're sitting right now—you can just take for granted that you're sitting. But when you close your eyes and feel the chair holding you, and you start feeling your surroundings, then it makes it easier, because you remove your mind out of the way. To me, the heart is always in tune with the time and the melody. But if you start to think about, "I wonder what key he is playing in," then you can't even tune your guitar, because you spend so much time calculating and fabricating and criticizing, that by the time you get to the song, they've finished already. But if you just feel, it's the most natural thing to do. If you just feel, you can create. I think music training would help me from the point of writing my own songs a little bit faster. Sometimes, it does take me longer, because what I hear I have to search for in different positions until I find it, instead of saying, "I think what I hear is a D-something."

Do you mainly write songs by trial and error?

Yeah, I just hear something, and I have to look for it. A lot of times, I don't have to look for it—I just find it. Other times, what I'm finding is— since I'm getting away from three-chord progressions or G minor to D

major kinds of things—you have to use so many chords. And it's just natural to be a product of what you hear sometimes in your environment,
like Stevie Wonder. I'm hearing more harmony, so it takes me a little bit
longer now.

**When you hear an idea for a song in your head, is it usually a melody or a set of
changes or a rhythmic motif or what?**

It's a cry. It's a crying melody. That's mostly what I hear, and then I
have to find the chords. Sometimes, it's the other way around, and one
chord could almost make up for three melodies. But, sometimes, the
melody is so clear, you want to find three passing chords for that melody.

**Your guitar solos seem to stay pretty close to the melody of the song itself, as
opposed to players like, say, Al Di Meola or John McLaughlin, who use a lot of scalar
things. Are you thinking of the song's basic theme throughout your solo?**

Yes. To me, the heart of the song is the melody. And I approach the
melody from a singer's point of view—a simple singer, not a singer who
scats a lot like George Benson. If you'll notice, a lot of guitar players riff
like horn players. And I don't really like guitar players like that. Not that
I dislike them with a passion, but it doesn't appeal to me—it's boring. I
think more like the layman kind of person singing [*sings*], "Lovely Rita
meter maid . . . ." You don't care what chords are underneath—it's the
basic feeling of the song that gets you immediately. I listen to the radio
a lot, so I don't think like "deedleedoodah" and that sort of thing. And I
figure, why do I like that when there are so many thousands of cats who
can do it a zillion times better? That's what they are, and I just get into
what I am now. It's like your signature. This is a very valid point for me
now. Some people may think it's negative, but I think it's positive,
because I am aware that out of thousands and thousands of guitar players, there are only, like, 30 who you can listen to and know who they are.
The rest all sound the same—at least that's what I think. And it took me
a while to realize that that's a very beautiful gift—your own individuality—even if you only know three notes, man, if you are able to play
those well, and know who you are. I don't think I was aware of my sound
until three or four years ago. Even when I did that album with
Mahavishnu [*Love Devotion Surrender*]—after a while it was, "Gee,
who's playing what?" It even took me a while to figure out who was

doing what, because we were playing so many notes that, after a while, the sound was all the same. Then I started hearing a certain amount of chops, and I said, "That's Mahavishnu." Then I'd hear three notes and say, "Well, that's me." I think it goes back to when I was listening to Johnny Mathis and Dionne Warwick and playing behind the melody, rather than doing what the trumpets and horns or somebody else was playing. I really didn't listen that much to bebop. I missed that era. I was into all these blues people like Jimmy Reed who only play three notes, but they grab you. As far as I'm concerned, the point of music is to tell stories with a melody. All that stuff about playing notes, to me, is just like watching some cat pick up weights. After a while, who wants to see somebody flex their muscles?

Your guitar playing is extremely vocal-like in tone and phrasing, yet you've never been the lead singer of the Santana band. Do you try to compensate for that in your playing?

Right. I think that's exactly it. I sing through the guitar. The main theme is always haunting melodies.

Your sets in concerts are almost like concept albums in that there are very few breaks between songs, and the transitions from mood to mood are very subtle.

Yes, it's the mood. I learned that from Miles. He goes through an hour-and-a-half, and it's like showing you a whole desk of beautiful jewels and just looking at them without breaking the continuity. Like, "Okay, I'm going outside to put a dime in the parking meter." You just sit there, and, all of a sudden, it hits you like that. I think mostly I learned that from Miles—to put everything so that it's constantly transcending itself. You try to make it peak and resolve. Sometimes, we feel like we do have to pause and let the people, like, gulp it in and digest it for a while. But I like to go from song to song to song. It's more fun.

Is *Lotus* [Santana's triple-set import] ever going to be released in the United States?

I don't think so, because they want to condense it into one or two records, and that would destroy the whole thing. That was all one concert, you know. We recorded that in 1973, in Japan. We were playing close to four hours in those days. But you can only play for so long like that. It's like giving people too much food, instead of giving them a nice portion so they don't start yawning and falling asleep. But we don't like to break, because then you lose momentum. Whereas, if you're already sweating

"IT TOOK ME A WHILE TO REALIZE THAT YOUR INDIVIDUALITY IS A VERY BEAUTIFUL GIFT"

you're getting into it. Once you stop, you don't want to start again.

When you were listening to Miles Davis and John Coltrane, was there any particular band or period in their careers that you especially liked?

Well, I identify with their music and them so much—not what they're about, but what's inside them. Not the personality. I don't identify with a part of the personality at all. But the creative and spontaneous musician, I totally identify with him and everything that he does. Sometimes, I wake up and start listening to Miles' quintet when he had [drummer] Tony Williams [along with bassist Ron Carter, keyboardist Herbie Hancock, and saxophonist Wayne Shorter], and I can just go through the day. Other times, I can listen to it, and I don't get as much out of it as I would from, say, when he had [percussionist] Ntume and [bassist] Michael Henderson. It depends on what kind of mood I'm in. I love all of it, and I can relate to all of it. The only period that I really can't get into still is the old, real cool jazz and bebop with [alto saxophonist] Charlie Parker. It still takes me a while to get into that. I put it on, and it's like being a little kid and somebody puts on Guy Lombardo. When you're a kid, you don't want to hear nothing like that. You want to hear Mickey Mouse, or maybe Chuck Berry. So with this kind of music, I don't think it's really over my head—I just don't think it's my style. I try to listen to it as much as I can, but, after a while, I can't relate to it. I can listen to [pianist] Thelonious Monk more than that, but in some of the other stuff there's too many riffs for my taste. But then I'm not a bebopper.

What about Miles' later period, beginning with, say, *Bitches Brew*?

I can relate to it, because being into airports and being into New York streets, I could see where that comes from, and I begin to love it, because I've been there. I've been through all that. It's like someone flashing you a year of New York in 25 minutes, and they pick the best outrageous scenes and put them to music. Miles is an incredible storyteller of outrageous, funny things.

Have you ever met him?

Yes, I've met him a couple of times. We've done a few concerts together. I begged Bill Graham to put us on the same bill. We did a couple of concerts at the Fillmore when he had Chick Corea and Keith Jarrett, and I couldn't believe the audience's response.

Did you ever have occasion to jam with him?

No. One time, he invited me to play in this club, and, like a fool, I said no. He kept pressuring me to go get my guitar. I kept looking him straight in the eye, and I was so insecure about my playing at the time—I think because of the dope. If I had been aware of what I'm aware of now, I would have said "sure." I should have trusted my ears to know what to play and what not to play. But, at the time, I was so paranoid. But that feeling was valid, because most rock and roll musicians that I know get paranoid when they see a jazz musician. You feel like those guys are older brothers. It's like being a kid, and your brother tries to get you to swim on the deeper side of the pool, and you don't know how to swim that well [*laughs*].

Is there anyone today who you'd be afraid to jam with?

When I have a good meditation, it would be pretty hard for anyone to intimidate me, or for my own mind to intimidate me, because then I'm in my heart. If I was in my mind, anyone could scare me. When I close my eyes, I completely identify with Joe Zawinul and Chick Corea and Herbie Hancock and Wayne Shorter and people like that. No, I don't think I would be intimidated if I felt at one with myself. I was really surprised when they told me that George Benson had chosen me to play with him on TV on *The Midnight Special*. I was really honored. In fact, I was overjoyed when I did talk to him, because I found out that success has changed him so much for the better. He's become more aware that people are listening to him. A lot of jazz musicians play in small clubs, and they couldn't give a heck who's listening to them. They just play, and they play incredible stuff. But, to me, the first duty is to make people relate and have a good time. It's like a mirror—you start feeding off each other. One time I saw George, and he was playing a little more to himself than to the people, and to me that's disrespect, because the people paid, and they feed you. I don't care what anybody says, if you want to be a musician, it takes two hands. One is to feed yourself, and one is to feed the people. But the last time I saw George Benson he was so incredibly receptive to the people. He had become warmer. It was really nice.

When you two played "Breezin'" together on TV it seemed to come off especially well because your styles are so different, yet complementary.

"IT TOOK ME A WHILE TO REALIZE THAT YOUR INDIVIDUALITY IS A VERY BEAUTIFUL GIFT"

Yeah. One time, I saw another guy who was incredible. I couldn't believe he could play like he was playing when he jammed with George Benson. It was Glen Campbell. I said, "Wait a minute!" But it's interesting to never underestimate any musician, because everybody has a heart, and when they become one with the heart, man, they can scare you. They can just play two or three notes and say so much. Jamming with George was very significant to me because he was very courteous to me. Some jazz players try to make you uncomfortable. They have the attitude that rock and roll guitar players—"What do they know?" George made me feel very comfortable, and that's what you have to do with musicians to bring out the best in them—make them comfortable. I think George has become aware that there's something extremely valid in the Beatles and the Beach Boys and Chuck Berry. It's just as valid as Charlie Parker and John Coltrane, only in a different way. God flows through everybody and everything, and that's what you have to realize. I think that's the best thing that crossovers are doing to people—making them aware that, "Okay, far out. Nobody can play jazz the way you can, but try to get into a straight B. B. King shuffle and swing it like B. B. swings it." You're going to have a hard time, unless you're open to that kind of music.

Have you ever seen or gotten into any guitar battles onstage?

I don't like that kind of pressure. I used to hang around the Fillmore and see a bunch of guitar players come up to B. B. King like they were gunslingers. You could see in their eyes that they wanted to burn him. And B. B. would just come out with some Django Reinhardt or Charlie Christian licks, and then after that play some B. B. King. I'd just laugh at the looks on those other guys' faces. When I went on tour with Mahavishnu, we did about 12 concerts together, and for about the first six, I think I was really intimidated by him. After that, I started seeing how people were waiting for me—like, they'd had enough of him. And I said, "Well, maybe I do have a position where I'll say something and they'll listen." I was intimidated until I saw people being moved by what I was playing. After a while, we gave some concerts together with acoustic guitars, and it's like anything. If you remove your mind, you can give someone a good run for their money, and you can even scare yourself, You just have to go inside yourself. If you spend your whole time thinking about what you're going to say, it's gone. You don't have time when you're onstage—you have to just go within and hear and feel and play. One time, B. B. invited me to play with him and Bobby Bland at Winterland. I was backstage, and, all of a sudden, he announced me, and they put the light on me. I walked out there with my eyes about this big, and he put his guitar, Lucille, in my hands, so I started playing. Growing up listening to those two, I felt like they were my fathers. I started playing, and B. B. and Bobby were singing, and old Bobby came over and put his arm around me. I have a picture of it, and I'm standing there with my mouth hanging open. I felt like a three-year-old kid next to those guys. To me, it was really significant, because they're almost like the forefathers of the blues. The blues is such a familiar part of me. I guess it is for most Americans, too. The first time Santana played in Chicago, believe it or not, the show was Led Zeppelin, us, and Albert King in the afternoon, and then B. B. King, us, and Albert King that night. I was sandwiched between B. B. and Albert, and I said, "Great. As long as I don't play no B. B. King or Albert King licks, I'm going to be cool." And I just played what I had from the Santana band, and, in fact, it was good, because playing this kind of almost Latin music in between two blues players was a perfect contrast. It went over very well.

What was it like the time you jammed with McLaughlin and Eric Clapton in Michigan?

That was a great one, man. See, Mahavishnu has this thing where you know when he's totally into his heart, because he gets into this little dance. And no matter where time goes, he is like the equator on earth—he holds it together. And he started playing all this stuff and dancing, and Eric yelled and took his solo, and then he passed it to me. Then I passed it to Mahavishnu, and we started trading around. Alphonse Mouzon was on drums, too. It was incredibly fun. It was a beautiful combination, really. One cat just elaborates on a ceiling kind of level—Mahavishnu, right?—and the other cat just plays two or three notes, man, with simple, hard power. And I'm somewhere in between. Eric Clapton is one of my favorite human beings of all time.

Did the collaboration with John McLaughlin come about because you were both involved with Sri Chinmoy?

"IT TOOK ME A WHILE TO REALIZE THAT YOUR INDIVIDUALITY IS A VERY BEAUTIFUL GIFT"

I was a seeker, and I still am a seeker. Even music is secondary to me—as much as I love it. Mahavishnu called me and said they wanted to know if we could do this album together, and he also wanted to know if I was interested in coming to see Sri Chinmoy. He felt that I was aspiring or crying for another kind of awareness, because, at that time, I had already made a commitment to close the book on drugs and booze and that kind of stuff. I just felt that it was like being in the same classroom and seeing the same people. I had to move on. Then I started reading books about India and about spiritual masters, and it inspired me to work harder. Some people call it ambition, but I call it inspiration. When you have that, it's like having a different kind of energy—pure energy—a different kind of fuel. Sometimes, it's totally in this center of creativity, and it just flows through you, and, all of a sudden, you don't have to worry about who's going to like or dislike it. When it's over, you feel just like a bee. You don't know why you did it, but, all of a sudden, you've accumulated all this honey. So that's what brought us together. We had the same cry for the same purpose. But I did learn so much from him. He's an incredible musician. Of course, you always find the number one guitar player that you never heard before—someone who's probably never been recorded—but since I don't know him yet, Mahavishnu, George Benson, and Pat Martino are probably my favorite guitar players.

That seems odd, since their very technical guitar styles are almost the antithesis of your melodic style.

Well, I don't listen to them as much anymore—that's why I can say they're my favorites. The people who I listen to a lot are my favorites in another kind of way, because they're so close to me. I put them in another category. The people that I'm really close to, I don't even consider them to be guitarists. I consider them to be more like painters. But Mahavishnu and George Benson and Pat Martino are definitely guitar players. B. B. King doesn't seem like a guitarist to me—he seems to cry and play the blues and that kind of stuff. So when I hear him play, I don't even hear a guitar—I just hear this cry. If I was really into guitar players, I would say Django Reinhardt was really a "guitar player." He had both—he could cry with the melody, and then scare you to death with a couple of runs. He had everything. When we were first playing in

Haight-Ashbury at the Straight Theater, this friend of the band brought me this album by him and said, "This is who you should listen to, because you remind me of him." And I listened, and was totally blown out. He could play runs like a horn player, a piano player, or a guitar player, and then play some sweet melodies. And then when they told me he only had two good fingers, I really flipped.

Do you think the LP with Mahavishnu worked musically?

Yes, but our intentions weren't to bring any music together. Our purpose was to make people who are on the edge—like we were—of pursuing a different awareness, seeking a different goal, become aware. That was our purpose—the core of it. It wasn't really a commercial or musical piece.

How much do you think the music of Santana has changed over the years?

Well, it changed, because in the beginning I was flowing with [keyboardist] Gregg Rolie and everyone who was affiliated with the Santana band, so we were all a collaboration. We'd write everything together. We'd all put our two cents in. Later on, I found myself writing more alone, and it just took a different kind of route and purpose. I don't think it changed what I'm about drastically, because what I was always about—even when I wasn't aware of spiritual values—was that I really wanted to have people dancing and enjoying themselves. Forget about the rent and all the other problems and just have a good time. I feel like that's my primary motivation—to inspire people. If they want to dance, fine. But the other way that it did drastically change was that—instead of the Beatles and Jimi Hendrix—I got more into John Coltrane and Miles Davis and Mahavishnu and Weather Report. It's like what you eat is what you are after a while. It has to affect what you play. But it's like everything—you try something, and then you go back to what's natural to you. And with all that music around you, why not listen to it and see how somebody else reaches a song? But now, I'm back into dealing with what's more natural to me, instead of struggling in different kinds of music. I mean, it's still a struggle to get into my own sound and own individuality that God gave me. You always transcend yourself no matter what you play. But, at that time, I was struggling a little more, because it took me hours and hours. I would even sleep with a tape recorder on. I bought a tape recorder that would play both sides continuously, and I'd listen to John Coltrane all the time, because I couldn't understand the later albums. They were so hectic. Then, all of a sudden, it wasn't hectic at all. It was so sweet. It's like everything. You have to condition your mind to see that there's crying children in it, the love and compassion of a mother in the notes. The most significant thing that I learned in my whole life about music is the consciousness of it. It's like if you go to a bar where Elvin Bishop is playing, there's a certain consciousness he puts out. It's almost like being in a barn where there are chickens and pigs, and it's a very beautiful, happy atmosphere—very down-to-earth. Whereas if you go to a church or, say, to India, every music has its own consciousness. Music becomes like an empty glass, and whatever you put inside is the consciousness. If you play country and western or Brazilian samba or whatever, that's just the shell. It's how you feel—what you put inside the music—that's really significant.

"I forget that I'm maybe a significant figure in the world of music, and I become like a child who doesn't know anything except that I'm crying for spiritual values."

Around the time of the *Amigos* album a lot of articles came out stating that you'd "come back home" to the kind of music the Santana band had started out playing. Was that a conscious decision, or had you just absorbed different influences?

It was both. At the time that Jeff Beck came out with *Blow by Blow*, I was seeing the last of the musicians who got into the Mahavishnu thing, and I said, "Man, I'm ready to move on to something else." Why should I keep listening to John Coltrane and trying to play like that? So I went to New York and started listening to Latin music again, and I started listening through a lot of people's ears—how they listened to the first three Santana albums. I started learning something about myself. Even Earth, Wind & Fire and a lot of people gained something from the

Santana band's approach to music. So if they were willing to even say in an interview that they learned something from us, I figured, "Well, what the heck am I doing looking for something else? Maybe I already got something within myself—my own individuality." That's when I started getting into the room with the tape recorder and separating my playing from all the other musicians. Then I started realizing that I like Latin music and the Beatles and Eric Clapton, and that I shouldn't live in a world of nothing but Thelonious Monk and Art Tatum. Some might think that's a whole galaxy in itself, and it is. They're all great, but why limit yourself to a certain standard?

Did you notice the music affecting the audience in a different way?

We went for a year without a vocalist, and we were just playing as avant-garde as we were ever gonna get—like some things on *Lotus*. But, after a while, I started seeing people yawning, wondering when we were going to play something they could tap their feet to. You know, it was going a little bit over the ceiling, so I said, "Wait a minute. Maybe I should try to make a bridge and not be so drastic." Although I was having fun at the time, it's no fun if you're alone. At least for me, it ain't fun if you're trying to play basketball and all the other guys are on the other side of the court, and you're over here with the ball [*laughs*]. So Tom Coster and Ndugu [Leon Chancler] did a little bit of research on the band, and picked up what people sort of liked about the old band, and they started arranging songs like that. But I don't think that until the last album, *Moonflower*, has everything felt more natural to us. We don't have to go back to the first three albums to write like that anymore. We just get together, and it starts happening.

With a song like "Europa," which is very emotional, is it hard to play that night after night and still feel it as deeply as you did when you wrote it?

It's not as hard as it used to be, because I learned a trick to it, a way to condition the mind. I used to listen to B. B. King and say, "Wow, it took me forever to learn that riff, and I still don't have it down pat the way B. B. hits it." Then, after I saw him play, I could see that he'd make a certain face, and then hit the note. Every time he made the face like that, he'd hit the note. And I figured that he would go back somewhere in time to a certain place or somewhere inside himself and then hit the

"IT TOOK ME A WHILE TO REALIZE THAT YOUR INDIVIDUALITY IS A VERY BEAUTIFUL GIFT"

note. So that's what I do now. I forget that I'm maybe a significant figure in the world of music, and I become like a child who doesn't know anything except that I'm crying for spiritual values. I don't have to fabricate any grandeur trip or anything. It's like I'm very, very natural—which is what a spiritual master does. I think of Sri Chinmoy, and it makes it easier. I don't have to think, "Jesus, Al Di Meola is out in the audience," or any of that kind of stuff—all that pressure. I just feel like I'm playing for my guru, and instead of all those people around it's just one person, my spiritual master. I keep a picture of him next to the monitor.

Your father Jose plays violin?

Yes, and he sings Mexican folk songs. My father is like mariachi-type music. I'm doing this solo album called *Oneness: Silver Dream, Golden Reality*, and my father is going to be on it, and my wife, my brother Jorge, Narada Michael Walden, and my father-in-law, Saunders King. You know, I think it was in *Guitar Player*, they asked B. B. King to name his favorite guitar players, and one he mentioned was my father-in-law, Saunders King. He plays tremendous R&B guitar. I can pick up where Wes Montgomery and Kenny Burrell heard things from him. His sound is very big, fat, Rolls-Royce classy—not just fast chops. In fact, he doesn't play that much. He plays a couple of lines and then rests. But it's what he says. We played together at the Old Waldorf [in San Francisco]. He opened for us. It was an incredible experience. That's going to be a very interesting album, because it covers such a range of music with people who are very close to me. Like, I want to mix my father's Mexican music with Cuban music—you know, with mariachis and all the strings and then bongos and congas, too. And my father-in-law sings so sweet. I can't even think of anybody who he sounds like. It almost sounds like a high, soulful combination of Eddie Kendricks, Nat King Cole, and Billy Eckstein. It's very unique.

What kind of gut-string guitar do you play?

It's a Yamaha. I just endorsed them, and I'm really happy I did, because they go out of their way to make good instruments. The reason I left Gibson was because I feel like they're like McDonald's now. They just wrap a hamburger and throw it at you. There's nothing individual about it. Whereas Yamaha, to me, is more like my wife at Thanksgiving.

She spends a whole day in the kitchen just to knock you out with the food. She puts effort and time and love behind it, and you can feel it. People might think I'm crazy, but you can feel it when you pick up that guitar. You know whether or not somebody put something of himself into it with his hands. And Yamaha has that in their pianos and guitars. They're ambitious. They want quality.

Was your Yamaha electric built to your specifications?

Yeah. It's almost shaped like a Yamaha SG body, but it's really fat like a Les Paul. It has more frets, and for sustain I asked them to put a big chunk of metal like a grand piano right where the tailpiece is. You hit it, and it's like hitting an acoustic grand piano—it really resonates. When Yamaha first approached me, the guitar felt like a toy. You couldn't believe it—it was really light. You couldn't get nothing out of it. The frets were really thin. It just didn't feel like a guitar. It was like something you'd get in a hock shop—really cheap. So I sat down with them, and said, "Look, I can't play the guitar, man. I hope you won't be offended, but I just can't play it. But if you make it more solid, and put more wood on it . . ." Now, I think they make them like that for a lot of people.

Does the guitar weigh a lot?

It weighs a lot, although it's not too heavy. It's just heavy enough for you. When you hit the note, you don't have to use all those gadgets to sustain. In fact, I never use sustain pedals, and it really sustains better. Gadgets always make you sound like you're frying hamburgers through the amp. You have to find a kind of guitar that resonates.

There's some really nice acoustic work on *Amigos*. When did you get interested in that?

Well, my father had an acoustic nylon-string around the house, and that's how I learned Mexican folk songs. I noticed that when you play with the thumb, it gives it that sound synonymous with classical, or Spanish. There's a certain way of playing it. I don't know how to use my fingers—I use a pick on my thumb—but I heard enough Spanish music in my life, and I know what it sounds like, and I know how you can make it very emotional. If you've been to a Greek restaurant and seen those guys dancing, you know the emotional buildup. This is the same thing. I met Paco de Lucia in Spain, and I really got the chance to see

"IT TOOK ME A WHILE TO REALIZE THAT YOUR INDIVIDUALITY IS A VERY BEAUTIFUL GIFT"

what a real Spanish guitar player can do. It's such a beautiful art. I like him, because he's crossover, too. I'm probably going to get a lot of letters from people, but some guitarists put me to sleep. I have to have something that's close to me personally—what I'm into—and he is very close to me. He reminds me of Gabor Szabo. I like Gabor a lot—he's very expressive. The thing I like about Gabor is that he's a spellbinding kind of man. The way he stands is like a mongoose—it charms the snake and hypnotizes it until he gets it. Gabor does the same onstage with his music and his presence. He catches the groove, and you forget where the floor is and where the drink is, and he just engulfs you and drenches you with his presence. And Paco de Lucia has this, too. He starts playing, and you forget that you have arms and legs—you just become his feelings.

When did you start using the Mesa/Boogie amp?

My brother Jorge turned me on to that. I was in New York, and I was really unhappy with my Fender Twins. It gave me headaches just to try to sustain. When Leo Fender left the company, he took something with him, because almost overnight I couldn't get sustain from the new Fenders. Jorge came over and said, "You got to try this amp." And it really looked like the Tubes' amplifiers. It had a snakeskin kind of cover—really cheesy looking [*laughs*]. But, man, it sustained like crazy and was pure. So I never gave it back to Jorge [*laughs*]. I left him on the road without it—but I think he had another one. After a while I met Randy Smith [of Mesa Engineering] and I endorsed them. I'm sure that we started something, because Mahavishnu and Chick Corea and George Harrison and Elton John and everybody are playing them. The beautiful thing about it is it has three volume controls.

How do the controls work?

Well, if you want to practice really fast like Allan Holdsworth plays, you can still have that edge like you're bowing a violin—sustaining like that. Or you can play soft enough where the guy next door won't even hear you. By putting the first knob on the left on 10, and then the master on 1, you sustain like crazy, and it's about as loud as I'm talking right now. Or you can put the master a little louder and bring the other ones down, and you can play at the Berkeley Community Theater. But I never play with any of them above 7 1/2.

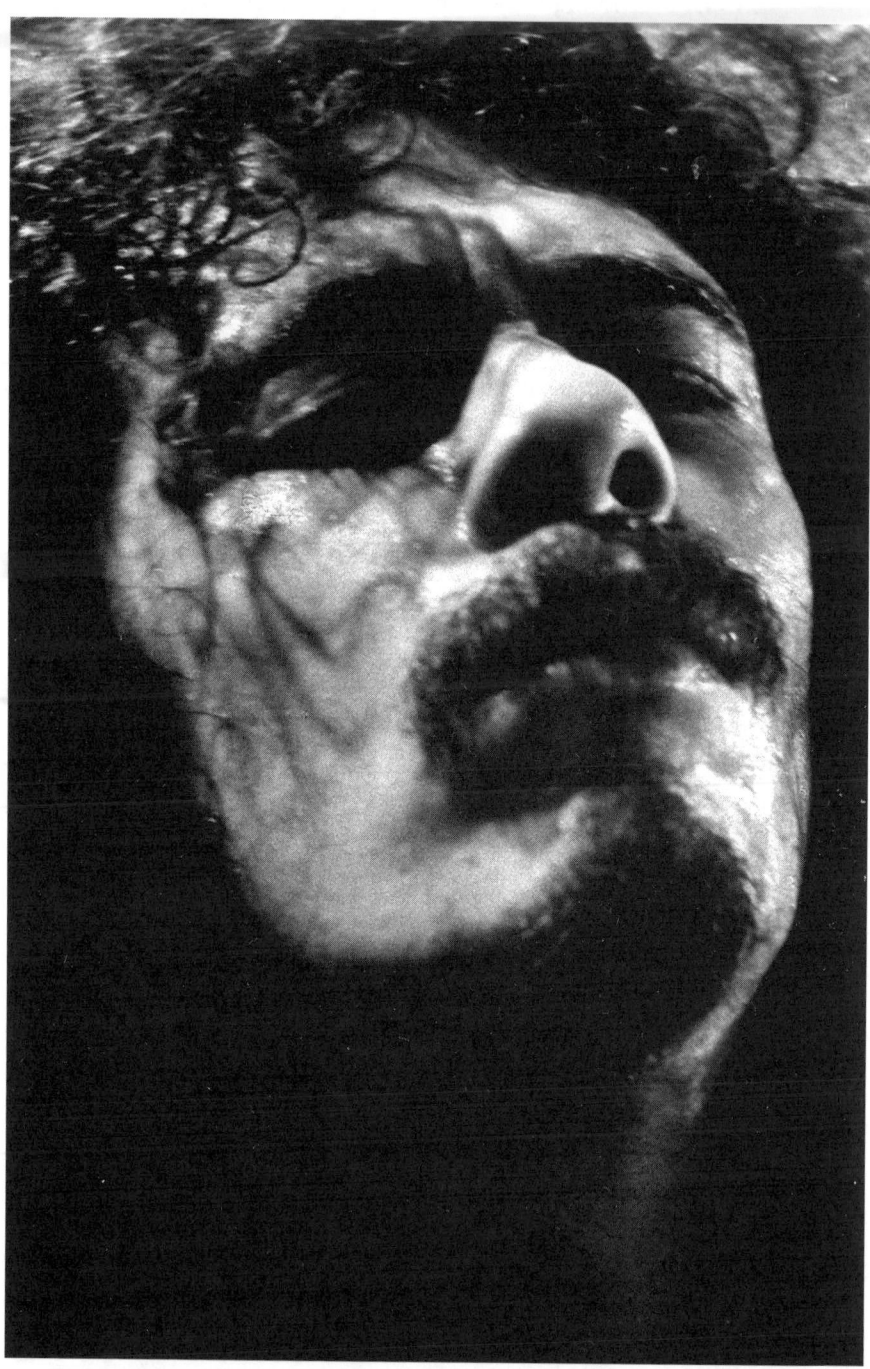

The Rapture: Santana channels his muse at San Francisco's Fillmore Auditorium, 1970. (©20TH CENTURY FOX / PHOTOFEST)

Not even onstage?

No, all three volumes are at 7 1/2, and that is really loud, and I don't even have them put me through my monitors.

What other controls are on the Mesa/Boogie?

Treble and Bass, and it has another one called Gain, which I put on 7 1/2 or 8. And it has a reverb and this Presence button that you turn on, and then pull the three volumes, and you get even more edge on it. I don't use that unless I'm going to play something really 1960s psychedelic. I don't like too much fuzz, but it's there if you want it. It also has a graphic equalizer, but I don't use that much. I use it in the studio, but not onstage.

What are your tone settings?

The Treble is at 7 1/2, and Bass is, like, 1 or 2. I don't like too much bass. Fred Meyers [Santana's sound man] did something where I'm playing through six 10s just by flipping a switch. Then I flip the switch, and I go back into the Boogie output. But the Boogie with one 12 is enough. When I play through the six 10s, that's when I play rhythm—it's clean and naturally gives you a lot of bass. I don't know how the Mesa/Boogie came about, but I remember going to Randy at Prune Music in Mill Valley, California, and saying, "Man, I wish somebody would come out with a volume that I could sustain at any kind of level." And he said, "Man, you're dreaming," or something. Then, all of a sudden, he had three volume controls. He's a very remarkable man, and I think he beat a lot of people to the punch. A lot of people still wouldn't think of that.

What type of strings are you using?

I use Yamaha strings—generally .008, .011, .014, .024, .032, and .042.

It's surprising that you get such a full-bodied sound with such a light setup.

Well, it depends on how high you put the bridge, too. The lower you bring it down, the more you can bend the lighter strings. But if it's higher, then it's more comfortable for me. Mine's not too high, but not too low. Sometimes, I feel kind of lazy, and I don't feel like really bending, so then I go to the acoustic guitar and start building myself up all over again.

Have you been using the Yamaha electric on your albums?

I've used it ever since *Amigos*. They made me another one—a beautiful green one—and it's better for ballads, because the pickups are original

Yamahas. I always change the pickups—that's the only thing that I change from Yamaha—but, this time, I kept them on. On the other Yamaha, I had Larry Cragg put in new pickups that he rewires, and the response is incredible. Larry knows what I want and what I need, and he goes for it. He really knows me, but I don't think he's ever listened that much to our albums. I've just been to his shop [Prune Music] so many times.

Do you still use the Gibson L6-S that you were using before the Yamaha?

Well, Yamaha came out with a guitar called a Super Combinator, and the body looks like a takeoff on a Stratocaster, but it has all those phases that the L6-S has. It sounds like a Telecaster, or like a Strat with the switch between the pickup positions. That's why I liked the L6-S—because it was a Gibson, but it sounded almost like a Strat. But I've got to tell you the truth: That guitar was like a General Motors car. Within two months, man, something would always go out. I found myself almost bleeding to sustain a note, and I know it wasn't all the amp's fault.

Before the L6-S you were playing a Les Paul, right?

Yes. It was a 1968 or '69 model. Neal [Schon] and I got them at the same time, but his got stolen. It's a very good guitar.

Have you ever played Fenders?

I play Fenders in the studio. Onstage I don't, because to sustain I have to play almost twice as loud on a Fender. See, I don't beef them up. I don't do anything to the pickups. And for sustain, Gibson humbuckers have always been hotter, from the get-go. On the other guitars, you have to have gadgets to sustain, or you have to play even louder, and I'm not ready to make the jump. But in the studio I use Fenders a lot. I played a Stratocaster on "She's Not There" [*Moonflower*].

Ever play hollowbody or semi-hollowbody electrics?

Yeah, I played a Gibson Byrdland on *Amigos* for chord work. But they might have mixed me out [*laughs*]. You know, it's incredible, because each guitar makes you play totally different. You don't even have to try, and the Strat will throw you into a different way of playing, like Montrose—really raunchy. But every time I play the Byrdland, I find myself playing more like Kenny Burrell. I was into him for a long time. When you play the Byrdland, you want to use the thumb more to get that beautiful tone. It's really solid for playing jazz guitar.

"IT TOOK ME A WHILE TO REALIZE THAT YOUR INDIVIDUALITY IS A VERY BEAUTIFUL GIFT"

What's in the rest of your guitar collection?

I have most of the ones Gibson put out, Yamahas, most of the old Fenders. Don Wehr [of Don Wehr's Music City, San Francisco] called me, because he had a real old Stratocaster in very good condition, and that's the one I play a lot when I record. But the rest just occupy space. Mostly, I just play the Yamaha now. A friend of mine, Linda Manzer, built me a guitar that has a great tone. Just recently, I got a new white Gibson SG with three pickups, because I wanted to get a tremolo. And it's mainly because I was listening so much to Allan Holdsworth, and I know that's what he uses. He's one of my favorite new players. I'd like to record one song with that kind of sound. Of course, I can't think or play like him. Certain notes and bends he does are extremely unique.

"Each guitar makes you play totally different. You don't even have to try, and the Strat will throw you into a different way of playing."

You've mentioned several artists as being crossovers, which is somewhat controversial, as some jazz purists no doubt resent a rocker like Jeff Beck winning this year's Playboy poll as Best Jazz Guitarist. In fact, the term "jazz" has been used by some to describe your playing.

And I'm not, right. I don't know why they classify certain artists like they do, but I'm not bothered by it, because I know that, first and foremost I'm an instrument myself trying to play something back to you. I don't consider myself a guitar player as much as I am a seeker who wants to manifest his vision through that particular instrument. I consider a guitar player somebody who sounds like a guitar player. In this day and age, it's hard to tell who's not a crossover, except Keith Jarrett. Even McCoy Tyner sounds like a crossover, although he plays acoustic piano. But the variety of songs he does—with strings or people singing—is a positive crossover. I don't consider "crossover" to be a negative term. Some players have used it just to make more bread, and their heart isn't in it, and that's prostitution. But somebody who is making an honest attempt to master another kind of music his own way is a positive crossover. I think the only one, to my ears, who day or night doesn't sound like a crossover is Keith Jarrett. But, to me, it's a challenge to learn everything on earth. One time, I felt like it was my duty to be a pioneer, but that kind of stuff I leave to someone else now. I don't care to be a pioneer, except for my own heart. But, consciously, I wouldn't make it a commitment to put that kind of pressure on myself. I just play whatever is comfortable without offending or belittling my instrument or my own integrity.

You said earlier that you don't play Latin music.

I mean strictly Latin music. If you listen to real Latin music, we don't sound like that.

What would you consider real Latin music?

Real Latin music is Tito Puente, people from Puerto Rico, people from Cuba, and some in Venezuela. Everyone else is a conglomeration. They hear something that sounds like Latin music, and they adapt it to their own style—like Gato Barbieri and myself. Which is a healthy thing. Like Blood, Sweat & Tears did on their second album with jazz and Latin things. Even Steve Winwood and Traffic put out some Latin things on *Mister Fantasy*. But it's not a real Latin sound—it's Latin *colored*. By me saying this, I feel that I really cleared the air to a lot of people—Latin people and any other kind of people. I don't want to be labeled like that, because I don't play like that. You know, if I wanted to play blues, it takes a long time to play the blues and really be known as a blues player.

Even though your original band was called the Santana Blues Band, you've never put a straight blues tune on any of your albums.

I only use blues for feeling. I think as close as I came to playing blues on an album was a song called "Practice What You Preach" on *Borboletta*. I always wanted to do a blues, but to play blues you have to have a blues keyboard player who can play like Otis Spann—someone like Alberto Gianquinto. He used to play with B. B. King, James Cotton, and Charlie Musselwhite. That cat is a monster. You can tell that his main people are Thelonious Monk, Otis Spann, Horace Silver, and Chick Corea—those are the people he's really into. I collaborated with him on

"Incident at Neshubar." I did the last part of it, and he did the 6/8 part and played piano on it. He helped us on the first two albums, because we'd never cut a record before. He said, "Look, all you have to do is take the fat out. Don't be going on and on, overstating anything—just pick the best part of the song." That's what we did. Otherwise, we would still be there [*laughs*].

Your first album didn't come out until 1969.

We were playing at least two-and-a-half years before we put out an album. That's how we got the reputation. We were headlining the Fillmore a couple of times, and we didn't even have an album out—you can ask Bill Graham. We must have been doing something right.

4.

"ERIC CLAPTON'S GUITAR IS A VOICE IN ITSELF"

. . . .

by Carlos Santana, July 1985

The first time I saw Eric Clapton was with Cream at the old Fillmore Auditorium in San Francisco. I didn't even know how they were going to sound, because *Fresh Cream* sounded so fantastic for being just three people. But they sounded *better* than the album the day that I heard them. They looked like giants—like they were on stilts or something. The music was overpowering. There were, like, three albums that came out that year—1967—that knocked everybody out: *The Doors*, *Fresh Cream*, and *East-West* by the Butterfield Blues Band.

The center of Eric Clapton's music—to me—is obviously the blues. But he has another plus—he is very lyrical. All of a sudden, his guitar is a voice in itself—or a trumpet, or an orchestra. He revolutionized a lot of things. From what I understand, even Jimi wanted to meet Eric when he first went to England.

Eric would crank it up, but he made it sound like music. A lot of other guys cranked it up, and it sounded like noise. Eric sounded celestial. I believe Cream opened the doors for a lot of bands, such as Tony Williams Lifetime, Jimi Hendrix, Led Zeppelin, and a lot of other people.

Eric and I toured together in 1975, and we got to spend time talking about things that we both love—blues players and things that inspired us. Boy, I learned from personal experience that Jimmy Page, Jeff Beck, and Eric Clapton—you can't back those guys against the wall. They have incredible arsenals of stuff. For example, we did a show at Nassau

Coliseum in New York where John McLaughlin jammed with us. Clapton waited for John to say his thing, and for me to say my thing, and then he came out with a switchblade, man. You know, he doesn't play fast, but like my conga player Armando Peraza says, "He gets inside the note."

I think it would be great to hear Eric in another setting—like with Brasil '77 or Jimmy Cliff—because what he has, he can't lose anymore. That identity will never be lost, but it would be interesting to hear it in a different setting.

A lot of other guys cranked it up, and it sounded like noise. Eric sounded celestial.

The last time we really spent time together was when Eric did the ARMS show in San Francisco. He hung out at my house, and I took him to Village Music in Mill Valley, and he bought a bunch of blues records. He gave me a tape with three or four songs that are not on his new album [*Behind the Sun*], and they're killer. One is called "Jailbreak," and another is "Heaven's Just One Step Away"—which is an incredible single, with reggae and stuff in it. I don't know why they didn't put those cuts out—they're happening!

5.

"THE MOST IMPORTANT THING IS TO LEARN THE ESSENCE OF THE SONG"

by Jas Obrecht, November 1988

The three-record *Viva Santana!* celebrates the career of Carlos Santana, presenting a mixture of earlier releases and previously unheard tracks dating back to 1968. To take the show on the road, Carlos reassembled his late-'60s lineup for the first time in nearly two decades. After two weeks of intensive rehearsals with keyboardist Gregg Rolie, drummer Michael Shrieve, and percussionist Chepito Areas, Carlos called on the eve of the tour to offer his views on the fine art of rehearsing.

How can musicians make the most of rehearsal time?

I think people spend a lot of wasted time on getting sounds together. They work for hours on their sound, and that stuff is never-ending, anyway. They MIDI to this and do that, and then when you tell them to play, they don't know the song. They should just rehearse with a plain, simple keyboard, one guitar, one conga, and just learn the songs. I tell people—and I don't care who they are—that it's important for them to spend more time knowing the changes, what the breaks are, and the transitions. When they go home, they can learn to MIDI and get their sound together, but the best way to utilize rehearsal time is to memorize dynamics, intensity, nuances, and things like that. I like to make sure that people know these in their dreams, so it becomes a very natural extension of transitions.

How do you teach them the songs?

*Santana onstage in the '80s—the same era in which he forged
a lasting relationship with PRS Guitars.* (© ROSS BARNATT / RETNA LTD.)

"THE MOST IMPORTANT THING IS TO LEARN THE ESSENCE OF THE SONG"

To me, the song is primarily the groove, which is the heart. If you have an incredible groove, who cares about the intro and the bridge and the end and the verses and the chorus? That's what I like the best about Talking Heads' *Remain in Light*. Those songs don't sound like songs—they sound like straight-ahead grooves. For new songs, I try to break it down so that people don't get too much cholesterol from either melody or rhythm. I try to balance it out, so that there's valleys and mountains, and it's not too frenetic. It's just like making love—there has to be tension and release, tension and release.

"As soon as you leave your house, you're at the mercy of all kinds of things. So I don't like to over-rehearse, but I like to rehearse enough so that everybody feels totally free and natural, and then we can improvise."

The main thing I teach people is the groove—you know, "This is how it goes." Let me hear what the drummer and bass player are doing, and then I bring in the congas. A lot of people can be a little bit too clever for you. They disguise what they don't know by just playing a lot. I say, "No, no, no. When I want you to play, really play it. But what I want you to really do is hold the groove." Wayne Shorter and I were talking about this. We want to lay a groove down that Wynton Marsalis to the guy with the green mohawk hair can get off on, because then we will hit everything in between.

What percent of rehearsal time should be spent actually playing music?

From the morning when you walk in until you leave. I feel like a fish in water, man, when the music is right, and that's what I try to go for in rehearsals. I can't stand it when people have to stop the groove a lot—it kills me.

How long is your typical rehearsal?

Usually from 1:00 to like 6:00 or 8:00. We take breaks to go eat and to discuss how things feel to people, whether somebody needs coaching, or if they need to know the breakdown on the song, how come the song works like this—that kind of stuff. I like to rehearse the band from eight to 12 days. Then, when we go onstage, we can just walk through it, even if the monitors suck or whatever. As soon as you leave your house, you're at the mercy of all kinds of things. So I don't like to over-rehearse, but I like to rehearse enough so that everybody feels totally free and natural, and then we can improvise. I always give the analogy that to rehearse is to know the corners, so you can always get home right. Once you know how to get home right, then you can take another route.

Do you typically update the songs at each rehearsal?

Yeah. With a lot of the songs, we have to. There are different musicians, and everybody plays differently. Nobody plays a shuffle, or even just a straight-ahead Jimmy Reed riff the same. The only people who play the way Jimmy Reed played it is Jimmy Reed and Philip Upchurch. The rest of us, we try to take some essence from it, but we're not going to play exactly like it. Ain't no way.

Should rehearsals follow the pattern of the show?

No, because rehearsal is only a schematic. It's a column of vertebrae. Once you get it, then you put the spirit on it. I try to put spirit anywhere—rehearsals and everything. To me, the most beautiful thing about rehearsing is when I can catch myself and the other guys in the band literally drooling. You know, when they get into the solo, you look up, and these people have gobs of saliva flowing from their mouth. You go, "Yeah! Yeah!" They're so blissed out and opiated with their own thing that they know the rehearsal was good for them. If they get lost, it's a good way to get lost—not in confusion, but imbued with the spirit.

What's the best attitude to bring to rehearsal?

The best attitude is to know that music should always be boiling—like boiling water. Whether it's soft or loud or fast or slow, it should always be intense. A lot of people play half-hearted when they play softly. They should never do that, because the spirit of the song goes out. The main thing is to not lose that intensity, and also to learn to project—not loud in volume, but to project.

Is it important to work with people you get along with?

"THE MOST IMPORTANT THING IS TO LEARN THE ESSENCE OF THE SONG"

Yeah. I'm professional enough that I can work with people that I don't get along with, but, first and foremost, music is harmony. If you only work with a person onstage—and offstage you can't stand his guts—there's no point, because all that stuff is going to come out onstage also. Some people are really good at masking their feelings. I'm not that way, so for me it's best to work with people who have respect for everybody in the band. Whether I'm onstage or offstage, I just don't want to be a psychiatrist or a cop or a nurse or a babysitter for anybody. I like people who can play the music and get along in the restaurant, too, and still complement life. That's what music is all about—to complement life.

How does it feel to be back with your old bandmates?

It feels great, because now after 20 years, there's a lot of mutual respect and admiration. They don't have to fight me like they used to, to be in charge of the band. I usually don't impose authority on anybody. I try to create the best possible setting so that every musician can express himself and bring the best out of the music and the other musicians. I believe that Gregg and Michael are comfortable with me now, and whenever they want to say something, I'm not going to stop them or block them. I'll say yea or nay, according to where they are. I go by people's eyes. I'll say, "Yeah, you're right. Let's do it that way," or "Whoa. Let's think about it overnight," or, "Let's play it, and see what it tells us." We have a better communication with each other now. It's not a do-or-die feel—like it used to be when we were kids. We can laugh at ourselves now.

You know, a guy came up to me in Jamaica earlier this year, and said, "Hey, man, I want you to listen to the baddest guitar player in the island." The first thing I said was, "Hey, man, do you know why the Lord created the world round? So we can *all* have center stage." That obliterates all that.

6.

"THE MUSICIANS I LOVE DIDN'T HAVE A PHD IN ANYTHING EXCEPT LIFE"

. . . .

by James Rotondi, January 1993

Carlos Santana believes in music—not just music's potential to amaze and delight, but its power to transform emotions, channel energy, and touch lives. The source of this power, the universal truth that connects Mozart to Monk, has been the subtext to the musical vision-quest Carlos began at age five, when he was first introduced to traditional mariachi music by his father, Jose Santana. Today, after 26 albums, Carlos hasn't lost touch with the humanity and generosity that inspired Eric Clapton to call him "the sweetest man I know."

If anything, Carlos' vision of the role he wants his music to play is clearer than ever. His newest release, the inspiring *Milagro*, is testimony to the strength of his convictions and the freshness and relevance of his singular guitar mastery. After 22 years with Columbia Records, Carlos recently signed with Polydor—a deal that includes the formation of Carlos' own custom record label, Guts & Grace. He remains a vital, explosive concert attraction and continues to pursue the fine art of jamming, sitting in with artists like B. B. King and Buddy Guy whenever the opportunity arises. The Santana band, featuring monster players like keyboardist Chester Thompson, bassist Benny Rietveld, and drummer Walfredo Reyes, is as strong as ever, and the accompaniment on *Milagro*'s "Saja/Right On" and "Agua Que Va Caer" supports some of Carlos' most lyrical and intuitive soloing.

Santana greets you warmly, without a trace of star affectation or suspicion. He speaks softly, with an earnest tone and a gentle sense of

Santana with one of his custom PRS models in the '90s.

humor. The admiration he feels for seminal musicians like John Coltrane, Jimi Hendrix, Miles Davis, B. B. King, and Bob Marley verges on worship, but one senses that it's enlightened respect, not mere awe, that informs Carlos' allegiance. After three decades of performing, writing, and recording, Carlos is not fooled by flashy gestures, technical overkill, or contrived feeling. He wants the real thing, because he is aware, as few are, that the right note in the right place can quite literally change lives.

"The first rule of music: If you don't feel it, why should they?"

THE LANGUAGE OF THE HEART

"The musicians I love, like Coltrane, Miles, Jimi, and Bob Marley—they didn't have a PhD in anything except life. If you told them they were legends, they'd probably look at you like you were stupid. The most important thing is to live life and tell the truth in a language of the heart. In the movie *'Round Midnight*, there was a guy who was following Dexter Gordon, and he said to Dexter, 'The way you played those three notes changed my life forever.' B. B. did that for me, and I'm sure I've done that for someone else. That's what's important. Bill Graham was the one who told me: 'Your music is a perfect balance of spirituality and sensuality, whether you accept it or not.' I'm not trying to exploit it, but I am trying to explore it. Most of the time, when we play in Texas or the Midwest, you'll see a guy with his hands clasped like he's meditating, and next to him is a lady with her eyes like she's having an orgasm, and with her hands she's saying, 'Come on, come on.' Her body is quivering. That's part of a concert—that's what should be in there, because music does all those things. The best thing is when you strip people of their hang-ups. There's a lot of people not too far from suicide or homicide. But music has the power to touch those people before they get to that point. When you make people cry and laugh at the same time, no matter what nationality or language they speak, you disarm them, and keep them from carrying those two hitchhikers that kill people—depression and frustration. To me that's very real, man. I got a letter as soon as John Lee Hooker's *The Healer* came out [*Carlos collaborated on the title track*]. This guy said, 'My wife ran away with this other cat. Life is too painful, and I had the knife ready to cut my veins. But I had the TV on, and 'The Healer' came on. Then I started to cry, and I started to laugh. I wanted to live. So I want to thank you for the tone, the message in the song. Because you and John Lee, you're the healers.' To me, that's what music is really for. That's the first rule of music: If you don't feel it, why should they?"

STREET UNIVERSITY

"I very rarely think of what chords, or what notes, or where I put my finger. You should have learned all the technical and physical aspects of the guitar in junior high school as far as I'm concerned. I don't think musicians who can really play think of music like that. When I'm playing a solo now, most of the time I'm thinking of combing my daughter's hair before she goes to bed, and I have to do it a special way so I don't make her cry by pulling her hair. Believe me, that's what I'm thinking lately, man! Unless I'm playing with Wayne Shorter. Wayne has an incredible way of writing everything. Those are the few times that I'm a musician with a short leash. If you read music, you've got to turn it down, and get to the paper, and get to what Wayne is trying to say. There are rules you need to learn when you play with Wayne Shorter or Joe Zawinul. You have to learn really quickly what they're trying to get across, and then make it your own. But to make it your own requires street learning. You cannot learn that in Harvard or Berkeley—you have to learn from the streets. The street university is very important, man."

BULLETS PENETRATING PAPER

"When people ask me to play on their albums, I ask them to send me a tape. I'll listen to the song first without playing a solo, and then I'll just go for what I hear. I know what chord I'm in, but I don't know what note I'm going to start with. All I know is a certain sound. If I hear country western or jazz or reggae, I hear a sound. Sometimes, it sounds like a baby crying in another room in the back of your mind. Sometimes, it

"THE MUSICIANS I LOVE DIDN'T HAVE A PHD
IN ANYTHING EXCEPT LIFE"

sounds like a bird, and, sometimes, it sounds like Jimi Hendrix's guitar coming at your face. Sometimes, it sounds like one of John Lee Hooker's moans. So then I try to capture that on the box. Usually, by trusting my hand, it goes right to what I heard. I think if I knew exactly what I was doing, I wouldn't have done it. A lot of times, you may hit some really ugly notes, but that's okay in the pursuit of that perfect thing. That's the whole romance of losing and finding yourself when you take a solo. You must lose yourself to find yourself. If you approach everything from an analytical point of view, the mind takes over. By the time you do your solo, it might sound great, but it's not going to penetrate. It will be like bullets that don't penetrate paper. There are a lot of guitarists with bullets that don't penetrate paper. Whereas other players—like Buddy Guy—they hit one note, and you see everybody fall out and go, 'Jesus Christ!' We've been jamming with Trey Anastasio from Phish [*who have opened many dates on Santana's current tour*]. I swear, he got so into his solo that a big ol' goo of saliva came over him and his guitar. He was drooling over himself like a baby. It was great! He looked up, and kind of cleaned up his slobber, and I said, 'Yeah, man—that's it!' That's the goal: to lose yourself to the point that Miles used to call 'a two-hour orgasm.' A spiritual orgasm onstage. That's what he'd wake up every morning for. That's a great goal in itself."

MUSIC IN BLOOM

"My time with Sri Chinmoy gave me some discipline, and an awareness of Eastern philosophy. But I look at it like my old tennis shoes from Mission High School. They don't fit me anymore. I came to him because of my fascination with John Coltrane and John McLaughlin, and I left him because of the same thing—my fascination with the spiritual side of music. I didn't go over there to join the Marines. I went because I was looking to clarify my feelings to an extent that when I play, it's as significant as a flower. Because flowers signify gratitude on Planet Earth—whether people look at them or not. When people say you should stop and smell the roses, it means that unless you identify with gratitude, you're always going to be miserable. At that time, when I got into Sri Chimnoy, everyone was dying, OD-ing left and right. So it was either the stuff they put in your veins, or fold your hands and give yourself to the Lord. I never wanted to become a casualty. I was afraid that I wasn't strong enough to shake off the same road that everybody takes, which was booze and drugs and 'I just play guitar so f**k everyone else.' Pretty soon, you see those people, like old boxers working in Las Vegas opening doors for somebody else. I didn't want to be a loser. What I like is clarity. I'm very simple. My mind is not complex like Frank Zappa or Wayne Shorter, so I always try to bring everything down to the most simple denomination, which is the heart.

"My father and I used to talk about the universal note, the universal tone. John Lee and Coltrane have that thing. Martin Luther King has that tone. I don't know why it is, but certain people are so powerful that when they speak, the soul stands at attention. That's 'Trane, Bob Marley, John Lee—just the tone. They could be talking about beans, it don't even matter. 'A Love Supreme' or 'Louie, Louie.' It doesn't matter. It's the presence they bring that makes it so strong."

SPIRITS DANCING IN THE FLESH

"There are very few musicians who can say something simple and soulful through a lot of chord changes, and not just run at the mouth. So what? I hear so many trumpet players who can play rings around Miles Davis in his last days. But two or three notes from him meant all of the chord changes, because he touched my heart. I listen to Charlie Christian a lot—and Django Reinhardt—but when it starts getting too complex and too dense and too thick with the chords, then what the f**k are you trying to say? Aren't you just trying to say, 'I love you? Whether you love me or not, I love you and the song is for you.' Isn't that what you're trying to say? Or are you trying to say, 'Dig how great I am, and I don't give a sh*t if you like it or not?' John McLaughlin, along with Pat Metheny, is one of the few musicians who can run all of it and make it sound 1992, instead of old like the '30s, '40s, and '50s. That's what I keep my ears open for: people who can run all those chord changes, yet I can still hear a child cry. I can still hear something human. Not just a typewriter. Who wants to hear a typewriter?

"I read books about how people in their 30s or 40s are just beginning

"THE MUSICIANS I LOVE DIDN'T HAVE A PHD IN ANYTHING EXCEPT LIFE"

to find out what their purpose in life is. I found that out when I was five years old, but it was reinforced when I heard B. B. King for the first time in 1966 at the Fillmore West. That's when I know I would be nothing else but that, no matter what. I'm very blessed. I'm very fortunate, because what I know I've known all my life, and that's all I want to know. I didn't want to know about algebra or George Washington's morals or wooden teeth or whatever. I couldn't wait to get out of school so I could go buy some John Lee Hooker records or Wes Montgomery records and tear them apart.

"Since Miles left and Bill Graham left, it really made me face up to the fact that time is short, and I have to get to the heart of what I'm trying to do. I learned the tools of the box when I was young. Now, it's just easier. I don't think of A, B, C when I'm talking to you. I don't think of consonants—I think of feelings. It's the same with the guitar. After a while, don't think of chords or progressions or time changes. You play what you hear. I get right to the main chorus, instead of walking around and nibbling here or there like I used to do. It gives me a lot of confidence, man, just to get to the heart of it, and get the hell out of there! [*Laughs.*] If you think, then forget it.

"What I'd like to do before I die is bring people closer to the same reality that John Coltrane and Bob Marley were trying to bring people to— no borders, one race, just one body, and we all take responsibility so nobody starves to death tomorrow morning. If you could do that with music, that's more important than becoming Hendrix or Beethoven, because you cause and affect the whole wheel of life in such a way that even though you are one person you made a difference—like Martin Luther King or Mahatma Gandhi. Then songs come like windows for people to look inside or look outside. That's why we love Jimi Hendrix. Because they're beautiful windows. When we look into them, we like what we see.

"So I'm more clear now as to why I'm doing everything. It's not just to make people happy or make them dance. It's to change things. Change myself, the people in my band, change people all around, so we can have a clearer vision about life and about ourselves, so there won't be as much disharmony in the world."

7.

"I PLAY RAINBOW MUSIC. IT'S LIKE DIAMONDS—ALL THE COLORS ARE THERE, BUT IT'S STILL CLEAR"

by Andy Ellis, August 1999

I had only one concern when making my new record," says Carlos Santana. "Would Jimi Hendrix like it if he were here? Would there be enough guitar? It's important for me to appease Jimi and Wes Montgomery because I play for them, too."

We're sitting in Santana's large rehearsal hall in San Rafael, California. Surrounded by bright wall hangings depicting his musical heroes—John Coltrane, Miles Davis, Jimi Hendrix, Charlie Parker, and Bob Marley—Santana is describing the genesis of his latest album, *Supernatural*. Featuring collaborations with an intriguing assortment of contemporary musicians, including Lauryn Hill, Wyclef Jean, Dave Matthews, Everlast, Rob Thomas of Matchbox 20, Eagle Eye Cherry, and the Dust Brothers, this release is Santana's debut on Arista Records.

"We're still finishing some tracks," Santana explains, as he cues up "Love of My Life," a song he co-wrote with Dave Matthews. "In fact, right after this interview I'm going into the studio to put some guitar on 'The Call,' which I wrote with Eric Clapton. It's time to put that one to bed."

As the punchy intro to "Love of My Life" emerges from the boom box, Santana's head bobs with the music. "You know what? There *is* enough guitar in there!"

Santana holds passionate views on a variety of subjects, and whether discussing songwriting, tone, and soloing—or such hot-button topics as spirit guides, self-validation, synchronicity, senility, and suicide—he presents his thoughts calmly, without a hint of rock-star posturing. Santana's speech is as distinctive as his playing, and he weaves his colorful tales of music and mysticism with unguarded sincerity.

Even if you don't share all of his beliefs, his ideas will get you thinking about the guitar and its role in our lives. Santana has survived more than three decades in the fickle music business without losing an iota of his enthusiasm for the 6-string and its great players. We can all learn from that.

Your new record is a remarkably collaborative effort. How did this come about?

Through meditations and dreams, I received these instructions: "We want you to hook up with people at junior high schools, high schools, and universities. We're going to get you back into radio airplay." I said, "Okay," because a lot of young people are not happy unless they are miserable. You can tell by what's happening at the schools. The vibrations of this music and the resonance in the lyrics will present these people with new options. I don't want them to feel like me or think like me—we're all individuals, and we're all unique. But with our music, we're presenting a new octave—a new menu. This menu says: "We are multi-dimensional spirits dwelling in the flesh, solely for the purpose of evolution."

You see, if you take the time to crystallize your intentions, motives, and purpose, and direct them for the highest good of life and people on the planet—behold, you get synchronicity. I'll give you an example. Working with [Arista label head] Clive Davis, we got hooked up with Lauryn Hill. She said, "Oh man, I love your music. Since I was a child, I listened to 'Samba Pa Ti'—I even wanted to put lyrics to it." So Lauryn invited me to play with her at the Grammy Awards. Playing with her was my first time there.

And what a night—she won five Grammys.

Yes, she cleaned up. Eric Clapton was in the audience, and he saw us perform. After the show, he called and said, "Look man, I heard that people at Arista were trying to contact me to play on your new record. I've

"I PLAY RAINBOW MUSIC. IT'S LIKE DIAMONDS—ALL THE COLORS ARE THERE, BUT IT'S STILL CLEAR"

been going through some serious changes in my life, and I was at a really critical point, but things are better now. Do you still hear me on your album? Is there room for me?" To hear Eric say that! I grew up listening to him, Peter Green, and Michael Bloomfield.

Then what happened?

Well, my spirits are Miles Davis and Bill Graham [*the impresario, not the evangelist*]. Even though they've left the physical world, they still come in my dreams and give me instructions. So when Eric asked if there was room for him on the record, I could hear Bill saying, "No, you schmuck, you're too late!" So I'm on the phone having a conversation with Bill and Eric at the same time. To Bill, I said, "Wait. Maybe you can talk to him like that, but I can't." And to Eric, I said, "Yeah, but you know what? I wouldn't think of dipping you into something that has already been recorded. Why don't you come over, and we'll write something from scratch?"

And that's how we started. We went through a couple of things and settled on something I had written, but never recorded. It has a Prince bass groove, but it's very swampy—you could hear John Lee Hooker or the Staple Singers playing it.

So that's synchronicity at work?

Exactly. Here's another example: Last summer, I asked an artist named Michael Rios to create a poster for us. I marked some passages in a few books and asked him to start with those ideas, and then continue with his own vision. Do you know what's really amazing? The images for lyrics that Dave Matthews, Everlast, Wyclef, Lauryn Hill, and Eagle Eye Cherry brought to the album are all in the poster! I didn't tell them to look at it or anything.

So I know there is something happening. It was like that from '69 until '73, and then it went somewhere else. Now it's happening again with this music. I'm in total awe of how fast and smooth things have been. Nobody has had a cow, nobody is bugged out—and there are a lot of producers, engineers, and artists involved with this record. They're putting their best foot forward, and all being very gracious. I keep pinching myself. I feel very incidental—I just show up, we see each other's eyes, we hear the music, and we start recording.

How do you describe your music?

I don't see myself playing black music or white music or gray music. I play rainbow music. It's like diamonds—all the colors are there, but it's still clear.

DAVE MATTHEWS
ON SONGWRITING
WITH SANTANA
BY KYLEE SWENSON

"We saw each other when we were both playing a festival in Germany," recalls Dave Matthews. "When Carlos was playing his set, he invited us to come up and play 'Exodus' by Bob Marley, and afterwards we talked about doing something together. We didn't really have a plan for what to do, just that we'd set aside five days to do it. Carlos had some music he'd been listening to that was inspirational to him, but when we got to the studio, we were just standing there with nothing but potential. As soon as he walked into the room, however, it was just joy. He threw his ideas out, and we came up with 'Love of My Life.'

"It's an incredibly simple song, which was an inspiration. He had the idea of reusing this Brahms melody, cutting it in half, repeating one part of it, and using the second half as a bridge. I'm always searching to make my life more complicated, but very often, lessons, inspirations, and moments of clarity come out of the simplest things. I think the most poignant moments in music are the most simple. Beauty doesn't always have to be complex.

"It's funny to think of the Brahms melody as it was originally. It's so different from what Carlos played—just changing the rhythm hid its origin. I love it because I can hear it so clearly, whereas if I were to play it for my mother and ask, 'Do you recognize the melody?' she probably wouldn't. He took that melody and turned it into a different piece of music. Just seeing how he put a song together opened my eyes to a different technique of writing. When I'm writing with the band—or by myself—I sort of wait for an idea and then put pieces together. But with Carlos, it's almost like he just sits down and builds something.

"Hanging out with Carlos was really enlightening. Even though he's such a heavyweight, he's an incredibly kind man. It was very pleasant to meet someone who spoke with so much knowledge and experience. I enjoy his analogies, his mixture of the mind and the heart, his beautiful parallels. Recording with him was like being away on a retreat as opposed to going into work."

"I PLAY RAINBOW MUSIC. IT'S LIKE DIAMONDS — ALL THE COLORS ARE THERE, BUT IT'S STILL CLEAR"

What's the process when you co-write a song with, say, Dave Matthews? Do you send tapes back and forth, or do you write in the studio?

There's a story behind that one. When my father passed away two or three years ago, I didn't listen to music for four days—that's a long time for me. I was picking up my son from school, and I thought, "Okay, time to listen to some radio." I turned on a classical station, and the first thing I heard was this melody [*gently sings a slow, six-note theme*]. The melody just stayed with me. They didn't say who the composer was, but I thought it was Strauss.

I wanted to find out what this was, so I went to the classical music section at Tower Records, and said, "All I have is this melody." I sang it, and the guy goes, "Oh yeah. Brahms Concerto No. 2." They get me the CD, and that's the song! I said, "Damn, you guys are good!"

So I brought this melody to Dave Matthews in New York. I said, "I hear this with a '1999' bass." I also recited these lines:

> *You're the love of my life*
> *You're the breath of my prayers*
> *Take my hand, lead me there*
> *With you is where I want to be*

Dave sat down and—bam!—wrote the song lyrics right there on the spot, and we recorded it.

Your guitar melody swings a bit more than the Brahms theme.

If Brahms were alive today, he would swing it, too, because it's what's happening. Listen to Dave's phrasing—he sang it like Billie Holiday or Frank Sinatra—way behind the beat. It's that human thing. Only squares sing in the middle.

As always, your guitar sound is very vocal.

When you listen to vocalists like Aretha Franklin and Dionne Warwick, you learn to phrase differently. For a long time, I wouldn't listen to guitar players—Joe Pass, Pat Martino, Jim Hall—because I felt that was another generation's music. I felt my music was blues and rock. But now, I'm discovering all this music by Jim Hall, Kenny Burrell, and Wes Montgomery, and it's like, "Oh, this guy is burning just as hard, but with a different fire."

I'm able to check out all the guitar players, take what I need, and still make those notes like Miles—you know, when you hit that note, you don't want to breathe until you finish with it. You go [*exhales*]. Miles, Peter Green—there are very few people who make you hold your breath until that note is ended. You literally feel like you've got a colic in your stomach. You get goosebumps. I love musicians who make you want to cry and laugh at the same time. When they go for it, you go with them, and you don't come back until they come back. [*Laughs.*] There are not that many players who can consistently do that. Potentially, we all should be doing it.

Were you listening to any particular musicians while working on this album?

I was listening to Peter Green, John Coltrane, and Miles Davis.

What were you listening for?

Peter Green for his legato tones. I mean, the first four or five years of Peter Green, because lately he plays more like Pat Martino. Staccato notes—John Coltrane. And from Miles, you get the alchemy of making 50,000 notes into five. But with those five, you shake the world. That was Miles' supreme gift. He could play two or three notes and, man or woman, you'd just go, "Oh, my God." Listen to *Sketches of Spain*. Play your guitar and try to keep up with the notes, the way he holds them, the breath of it. That's the voice of angels, man.

You see, great music comes not from thinking, but from pure emotion. As the Grateful Dead people say, "It's when the music plays you." You make the best music when you're not conscious of doing it. I've been saying these things since the beginning. I remember getting in trouble with Frank Zappa—I'm pretty sure he coined the phrase, "Shut up and play your guitar" for people like me, because we talk a lot! But I am passionate about turning on massive amounts of kids, and pulling them out of that miserable state. I want to turn them over. You don't have to be Jimi Hendrix or Charlie Parker—you can get it done in your own way. God made the world round so we can all have center stage. Everybody is important, as long as you're doing it from your heart. Frustration and depression lead to homicide and genocide, but inspiration and vision lead to a spiritual orgasm.

Can you describe this?

It's where you're constantly happy, and you don't have to feel weird when people say, "Man, what are you laughing about?" I'm laughing because I know the secret of life. And the secret of life is that I have validated my existence. I know that I am worth more than my house, my bank account, or any physical thing. When I hit that note—if I hit it correctly—I'm just as important as Jimi Hendrix, Eric Clapton, or anybody. Because when I hit that note, I hit the umbilical cord of anybody who is listening.

When you hit a note like that, people say, "What kind of guitar is that? What kind of speakers are you using? What kind of strings?" No, man. It's not all that—it's the *note*. Now, when you explain this to kids, they say, "Really? I can do that too?" Sure. We can teach you how to put five things into one note. [*To illustrate, Santana holds out the karate edge of his hand, and then rotates it to reveal his palm and five fingers.*] These are the ingredients for being a complete communicator: Soul, heart, mind, body, cojones. One note.

"When you feel that the world is not appreciating your genius, you're already setting yourself up to be a victim."

I validated my existence before I got out of high school. People would ask, "What are you going to do when you leave school?" I'd say, "I'm going to play with Michael Bloomfield and B. B. King." They thought I was crazy! I'd say, "Why are you laughing?" They'd say, "Man, you're tripping." "No, *you're* tripping because you don't know what you want to do. I know what I want to do, and I know who I'm going to be doing it with. And I'm going to play with those people."

Once you learn to validate your existence, you have the wind in your sails—where do you want to go?—and you can never commit suicide. I would say that as great as Danny Gatton was, he never took the time to validate his existence. When you feel that the world is not appreciating your genius, you're already setting yourself up to be a victim. There are a lot of musicians like that: "My manager ripped me off. My record company ripped me off. I'm going to eat beans, but I'm not going to play what they want me to play."

Which albums inspire you?

Tell everybody to hear *Spellbinder* by Gabor Szabo. That is a must for anybody who plays guitar. He's the person who I credit with pulling me out of B. B. King. B. B. had us in a headlock—Michael Bloomfield, Peter Green—we were all under his spell. Gabor played like a Gypsy, but different from Paco de Lucia. I first heard Gabor with [drummer] Chico Hamilton. The band had no piano player. It was just congas, timbales, and drums with Gabor and [bassist] Ron Carter. It sounded unbelievable.

So *Spellbinder* is one of those "Holy Grail" recordings?

Exactly. Also "The Supernatural" by Peter Green, Bola Sete's *At the Monterey Jazz Festival*, and Wes Montgomery's *Goin' Out of My Head*. Unplug the phone, sit down with these, and you're in for a real surprise.

If someone was searching for essential Santana, which of your records would you recommend?

For pure songs, *Abraxas*. For pure guitar, I would say *Caravanserai*. Neal Schon and I played really well on that album. At the time, the

SUPERNATURAL GEAR
BY ANDY ELLIS

According to renowned guitar tech René Martinez, Santana recorded *Supernatural* using Paul Reed Smith guitars strung with D'Addario nickel strings, gauged .009–.042. "The PRS pickups are specially wound for Carlos," details Martinez. "There's a Dragon humbucker in the bridge position and a Santana model humbucker in the neck position. Carlos also played a stock '57 sunburst Strat with a maple neck. For amps, he used a '70s Marshall 100-watt head and 4x12 cab, a '65 blackface Fender Twin, and a Mesa/Boogie combo loaded with a single 12" Altec. The Boogie has been with Carlos a long time. All these amps are in good condition, and they sound great.

"We placed the mics to reproduce the overall sound we heard in the studio and to capture the authentic amp tone," continues Martinez. "Carlos played through all three amps simultaneously. This way we were able to blend tones for each song. There never is a 'right' setting. You have to get into a studio and tweak the sounds for that particular room. For effects, Carlos kept it simple, relying on a wah, spring reverb from the Twin and Boogie, and a reissue Ibanez TS-9 Tube Screamer."

"I PLAY RAINBOW MUSIC. IT'S LIKE DIAMONDS—ALL THE COLORS ARE THERE, BUT IT'S STILL CLEAR"

Allman Brothers had two guitar players. I remember Miles was really upset with me because I had another guitarist, but I told him, "I think Neal is a great guitar player, and that's what I hear right now." I believe it worked. Later, Neal went to do his thing with Journey, and because I still craved to play with another guitarist, I played with John McLaughlin.

Once I got that craving out of the way, I wanted to learn why I was so fascinated with Coltrane and that "sky-church music," as Jimi called it. So I got together with [pianist and harpist] Alice Coltrane, and I found out why she writes, and how she writes those celestial strings. It's important for guitarists to listen to her and [tenor saxophonist] Pharaoh Sanders.

How do you write songs? Do you keep a tape recorder running to document your ideas?

All the time. I play for two or three hours and keep flipping tapes. I mark them, and then come in the next day and listen to them. After a half an hour, I might say, "Ooh—right there. Let me transfer this." I keep another tape recorder filled with little nuggets of all that rambling. That's what I present to Eric or Dave Matthews.

So it's a two-stage process—first you capture inspiration, then later you organize those magic moments so you can play them for people.

Right. That's what I've been doing since I can remember. It works for me. Late at night, if I want to check in with my internal Internet, I load the tape recorder, get some nice tones, and play. And sometimes it's okay to watch TV with the sound off. Maybe you're playing music to a car chase, and the next day you go, "What was I thinking?" Well, you were watching TV and putting music to it.

I'd be remiss if I didn't ask you about tone and how you got it on this record.

I'm very honored to be working with René Martinez, who worked with Stevie Ray Vaughan. René can play the hell out of the Segovia guitar. I should be his roadie! He told me everything that Stevie Ray went through to get his tone on tape. Amps all over the place—in the kitchen, bathroom, halls, and everything. Everybody has to find out what works for them.

What works for you?

Well, I bring my amps and microphones to every studio, because I found out that when you position certain microphones in a certain way, the room doesn't matter after a while. I have one microphone placed at the amplifier and another one positioned farther back so you can hear [claps] the ghost sound. You can't get that with knobs. They just give you an emulation.

As you recorded *Supernatural* in several different studios, was it difficult to get a consistent tone?

Sometimes, I would say, "Look man, you're giving me a snapshot of me. Imagine I'm a singer—you're only giving me head tones, nose tones, and throat tones. I want the chest tones and belly tones—even toe tones! Give me the whole thing. That's why I've got a Marshall." The technician might say, "I don't know what you mean." I'd say, "You want to know what I mean? Open the damn door." As soon as he'd open the studio door, I'd say, "Hear that sound coming in? I want that in the speakers. I don't want to sound compressed and chopped. I don't sound like that." Sometimes, I'll help place the microphones, and now I even bring my own engineer, Jim Gaines.

The only thing that I have is my tone. That's like my face. Your tone is your fingerprint and your personality. Don't mess with that. Otherwise, you can get anyone from L.A. who just does it with pedals and sounds like a beer commercial. That's okay for them, but I learned by listening to T-Bone Walker and Peter Green, so I have a tone.

You mentioned Marshalls. What amps did you use for this record?

I used Marshalls, Boogies, and Twins. I went through my six Marshalls and got rid of the ones that weren't consistent. Some you plug in and it's glorious. Some you have to babysit and change diapers and change tubes. I found the ones that are happening in the studio or a coliseum or anywhere, and I kept those. We mark them—these speakers go with this head. That way, you're not shooting in the dark. You know exactly what you're going for when you're recording.

Are you still playing your signature PRS?

Still the PRS, although with Eric, we both played Strats because I wanted to keep it even. It's such a pretty tone. Because of René, I finally played through a Tube Screamer. In the past, I always said, "I'll never use those things because I want to sound like me." I would just mark the floor in the places where my guitar sustains. When I'm onstage, there are marks for

"I PLAY RAINBOW MUSIC. IT'S LIKE DIAMONDS—ALL THE COLORS ARE THERE, BUT IT'S STILL CLEAR"

this song, marks for that song . . .

Do you mark the studio floor, too?

Oh yes. At first, I told René that I didn't want to play a Strat, because to make it sustain, I'd have to play so loud that I didn't know if I could have babies! So he goes, "You don't have to play that loud. Try this Tube Screamer." So we plug it in, and—bam!—it sustains right through a Twin or a Marshall. You can still talk, but you're sustaining furiously. I said, "Oh, I shouldn't have been so bullheaded. I'm so stubborn." And he says, "You didn't know. Stevie used pedals to sustain." I went, "No kidding? I thought he was just loud."

"The only thing that I have is my tone. That's like my face. Your tone is your fingerprint and your personality. Don't mess with that."

It has been a real education working with René. In fact, the entire process of making this album is new to me. Even though I've been recording since '67, all of a sudden, I'm thrown into a whole new way of doing things. I really like it—it's fresh and very challenging.

Any advice for fellow guitarists?

The last thing I want to say is that whether you play blues, bluegrass, or jazz—whatever—realize that when you get older, you either get senile or become gracious. There's no in-between.

You become senile when you think the world shortchanged you, or everybody wakes up to screw you. You become gracious when you realize that you have something the world needs, and people are happy to see you when you come into the room. Your wrinkles either show that you're nasty, cranky, and senile, or that you're always smiling.

That's why I hang around with Wayne Shorter, John Lee Hooker, Herbie Hancock—people who have passion. I've never seen them bored. I'm like a kid—I'm 51 years old, but I still feel like 17. I got the recent

Guitar Player at my house yesterday, and I sat down and read it. It's the only magazine I read from beginning to end, nonstop. Most magazines are very biased into one octave. Your magazine covers women and men, the gifted and the beginners, brilliant and crazy garage bands—all of it—and I relate to that. Whether you've got a green mohawk or a suit and a tie, it's still the same: Are you saying something valid? Are you contributing, bringing new flowers that we haven't seen in the garden?

I'm looking at the new guitars and new amplifiers like a painter discovering new brushes or mediums. That fascination with instruments and sound and texture hasn't gone yet. It's really fun.

SANTANA'S SETUP

BY GARY BRAWER

If you see Carlos Santana perform, you are sure to notice this Santana model PRS. This guitar—which he feels sounds and plays better than his other instruments—features a highly flamed maple top on a mahogany body with a mahogany neck and Brazilian rosewood fingerboard. The Gibson-esque 24$^{1/2}$" scale, 11$^{1/2}$" radius, and slightly larger-than-stock PRS .105" x .050" jumbo frets all add up to easy bending.

Santana's tech, René Martinez, likes to keep the stock PRS tremolo floating off the body because he feels it stays in tune better for dive-bombing. The neck is kept perfectly straight, and the string height at the 12th fret is $^{5/64}$" on the bass side and $^{4/64}$" on the treble side. The PRS Santana model neck pickup and the PRS Dragon II bridge pickup both have chrome covers. The bridge pickup is custom wound for a sweeter high end—as well as optimum feedback and sustain. The bridge pickup sits $^{3/32}$" from the strings, while the stock neck pickup is at $^{1/16}$". The volume and tone pots are 500k, and the volume pot sports a 181pf capacitor to preserve high end as Santana backs down his level. The unique switching consists of two 2-way mini-toggles, which perform as follows:

* Both switches up—neck pickup
* Both switches down—bridge pickup
* One up and one down—both pickups

Santana uses D'Addario nickel strings, gauged .009–.042. Martinez adds that the bottom line for his boss is simple: "The guitar must sustain and have great tone

8.

"YOU'RE WORKING IN A FIELD OF MYSTICAL RESONANCE, SOUND, AND VIBRATION"

by Andy Ellis, January 2003

The astounding success of Carlos Santana's *Supernatural*—which has sold more than 24 million copies since its June '99 release, and earned eight Grammy Awards (including Album of the Year)—has made fans wonder what the soft-spoken guitarist could possibly do for an encore. With his latest record, *Shaman* [Arista], Santana proves that his fiery licks and singing tones are, in fact, hotter and more vocal than ever, and that his collaborative instincts remain strong. Once again, he has teamed up with a small army of musicians, singers, and writers, including Macy Gray, Seal, Ozomatli, Nickelback's Chad Kroeger, Michelle Branch, P.O.D, Marc Anthony, Dido, Wyclef Jean, and, most surprising, opera singer Plácido Domingo.

While the teamwork is strong, the real action lies in the wall-to-wall guitar that alternately moans, wails, and rips through the 16 tracks. Ripe and tubular—and often accompanied by the audible thump of a beleaguered 4x12 cabinet—Santana's notes seem to spring effortlessly from his trusty signature PRS.

As always, the 55-year-old icon answers questions with a compelling mix of allusion and candor, and even if you take issue with some of his observations, they'll make you stop and think. Above all, his enthusiasm for guitar will make you smile, and his latest amplifier discovery will have you scouring basements, attics, and classified ads for one of ampdom's rarest beasts.

Like its predecessor, *Shaman* is a cooperative effort. Did you try to approach this project differently from *Supernatural*?

I'll use Wayne Shorter's beautiful words: "It was completely new and totally familiar." As before, I used six strings and an amplifier to find my way into the music. But I also took some advice from [Arista label head] Clive Davis. He said, "The dimensions of *Supernatural* make it so that many people want to play with you now. But I think we should concentrate on the songs. They're more important than the people at the moment. Once you find the right songs, then we can see who would be best suited to play them."

Like my brother Ry Cooder, I'm learning to navigate different routes. Before it was Hammond organ, congas, guitar, and, finally, songs. Now it's the opposite—it's songs and then guitar, Hammond, and congas. But I still don't think in terms of numbers and commercial success. I think of opportunities and possibilities. Working with Dido, Macy Gray, and Michelle Branch—and all these new people—I feel the same energy that I felt when I first heard Michael Bloomfield, B. B. King, or Son House. So I ask myself, how do I express this intensity of emotion and spirit without imposing on the song? The goal is to complement, and also to give some spiritual information.

As you know, the only magazine I read cover to cover is *Guitar Player*. I say this because you cover everything—woman or man, super fast or super slow, deep or shallow. You're not exclusively jazz or country or heavy metal. In this way, I feel really honored and grateful to participate in *Shaman*, because when you go from P.O.D. to Plácido Domingo, it's like your magazine—it's pretty vast.

What do you look for in a song?

I'd better be able to live with it for the next 10 or 20 years! When we were selecting songs for *Shaman*, I heard several that just weren't me. One was by Diane Warren, who has written humongous hits for Aerosmith and so many others. This song, with all respect, was probably written for John Cougar Mellencamp, and it was too far for me to reach. A song has to make it into the galaxy of Santana. If it doesn't, I don't care if it's a number one hit—I won't play it.

Throughout the album, your tone is remarkably clean and articulate, yet fat and sustaining. On "Amore (Sexo)," for example, did you use a dual amp setup to get that elusive mix of detail and girth?

"YOU'RE WORKING IN A FIELD OF MYSTICAL RESONANCE, SOUND, AND VIBRATION"

No. Early this year, I discovered a phenomenal amplifier made by Alexander Dumble. I'd heard that Stevie Ray used Dumble amplifiers, but I thought, "Sure, whatever. He has great tone anyway." As soon as I tried it, however, I heard Robben Ford and Larry Carlton in the sound. That's how I got hooked for life.

What draws you to a Dumble?

They're touch sensitive. Caress a note, and it goes soft. If you have mean intentions, and hit a note a certain way, the amp screams, and you get those seven overtones on one note. You know those supernatural sounds we always look for in Peter Green or Michael Bloomfield? They're right there.

Dumbles are rare. Where did you find one?

A gentleman named David Workman—a musician in the San Francisco area—lent me his. He said, "I want you to try this amp, but under no circumstances can you buy it. I won't sell it for any price, but you can use it in the studio and on the road." From there, I made the personal communication with Alexander Dumble, and that was it. I went from not knowing about Dumble amps to having four.

Has the Dumble changed how you work in the studio?

Sometimes, it used to take days just to get a tone. Even with the incredible [engineer] Jim Gaines, I was getting frustrated because my sound wouldn't happen in certain rooms. It's really depressing when you're ready to play, but you listen to the playback, and it sounds so horrible it hurts your teeth. I'd go home and think, "Maybe it's me. Maybe I can't play anymore."

The beautiful thing is that with the Dumble, I just plug in and play. I don't have to go through hours of placing microphones. We used the same setup at the Hit Factory in New York as we did here in California. Same microphone, same position. Bam!—there it is. You don't have to wrestle a wet bear just to get a tone.

Can you compare the Dumble to the amps you've used in the past?

Since '72, I've played through a Boogie amp with one 12" Altec speaker. With the Boogie, I have to turn the volume past seven-and-a-half to get the beautiful, warm tones. If I play under that, it sounds really wimpy and thin and annoying. Playing the Boogie is like being inside a light beam. If you stand in front of it, it's really loud, but if you move two feet to the left, you don't hear it.

With the Dumble, you can play at any volume—like at Sweetwater [a tiny club in Mill Valley, California] or the Berkeley Community Theatre or the Oakland Coliseum—and get all those overtones. With other amps, you have to open them up really loud to get the richness. Bring them down, and it's like a big balloon that's not inflated. Dumble? No, he's got balloons at any size you want.

And you're also using a bigger cabinet.

Yes, a 4x12. We found this gentleman who makes speakers with hemp cones [these are Tone Tubby alnico speakers made by A Brown Soun in San Rafael, California]. When I told this to Dumble, he cracked up. "Oh, I know who that is." They all know each other, these amp guys.

It's remarkable that you can draw so many timbral colors from one amp, from the bright, squawky leads in "Game of Love," to the sweet Peter Green bends in "Sideways," to the thick cello tones in "One of These Days."

Ah, you're listening. "Game of Love" was the last track I did with the Boogie before I found the Dumble. The rest of the album is all Dumble. People think that I'm crazy, but, one day, my Boogie amp got really jealous of the Dumble and broke down. "Hey, you've been playing me for 30 years. Why are you playing that other one?" I was like, "Shut up. Let's just work together." I got the Boogie fixed, and the amps made peace. Onstage, I use the Boogie and Dumble together.

Why?

Like a singer, you want to get belly tones, chest tones, throat tones, nasal tones, and head tones from your guitar. With its 12" Altec, the Boogie is a soprano. It gives me throat tones, nasal tones, and head tones, but not chest or belly tones. But now because I use four 12s with the Dumble head, I get the Pavarotti and Plácido Domingo belly tones.

Several songs on *Shaman* feature beautiful nylon-string guitar. Did you play those parts?

Yes. I used an Alvarez and recorded it with a combination of a direct signal and a mic. I love acoustic nylon tones. With all due respect to my brothers Paco de Lucia and Ottmar Liebert, the best acoustic nylon tones I hear are from B-Tribe. They do their own version of Concierto de

"YOU'RE WORKING IN A FIELD OF MYSTICAL RESONANCE, SOUND, AND VIBRATION"

Aranjuez, and they do a theme from the movie *Once Upon a Time in the West*. The way they hit the nylon strings is really mystical. Some musicians, man, you hear the note almost before they hit it. Jimi, Coltrane, and Charlie Parker were like that. Some conga players too—they raise their hand and before they hit the skin, you hear ta-duk.

What do you listen for in others' music?

You know "People are Strange," the Doors' song? Sometimes, you walk around, and it's this weird day and people look like old potatoes or apples. Their features are so exaggerated—even if you're straight. But then you hear a certain kind of music, and it makes everything beautiful. You remind yourself on a molecular level that there's goodness in everyone. Beauty, elegance, excellence, grace, and dignity—they're more important than what key you're in, or what chord or what scale you're playing. These qualities transcend what you learn in music school.

How do you translate these qualities into music?

You have to learn how to articulate emotion. When I first heard Jimi Hendrix, I thought, "My God, this guy has a different kind of brush." His was much thicker than everyone else's. They were using tiny little brushes and doing watercolors, while he was painting galactic scenes in CinemaScope. We're working in a field of mystical resonance, sound, and vibration. That's what makes people cry, laugh, and feel their hair stand up.

You play with many young musicians. Do they understand what you're talking about now?

I'm not judging anybody—it's just an observation at this point—but I can tell people's intentions, motives, and purpose from their eyes. I went to see Derek Trucks at the Fillmore, and I could tell that he's looking for the same things I am. I like Jonny Lang, because he puts so much pain and energy into his playing. Yet I see other musicians—I won't mention their names because I don't want to hurt their feelings—who act like they're posing in front of the mirror. They cop a tone in order to get something else. They're not going for the pure joy of creating a glorious sound like Otis Rush, B. B. King, or Buddy Guy.

Years ago you told *GP* readers that to find your sound, you'd play guitar for hours, alone in candlelight. Do you still explore the fretboard this way?

Oh yeah—every night when I'm not on the road. My family is on the school timetable, so after they go to bed, I play until 2:00 in the morning. I play with everybody I love, from John Coltrane to Wes Montgomery.

So you jam with their records?

Yes. When the inspiration runs dry, or I get stuck with too much cosmic music, I go back to John Lee Hooker, Jimmy Reed, or Lightnin' Hopkins. From those roots, I find my way back to Coltrane. Or I turn them off and just lose myself—and find myself—in the music. I'm not technically proficient, so I run a video camera while I play. That way, if I want to go back to a tone, I can see where that note is and what guitar and amp I used. When I view a tape two days later, it's like watching somebody peel an artichoke. You're peeling Peter Green, Bola Sete, George Benson,

SHAMAN SPELL

When guitar tech René Martinez (who worked with Stevie Ray Vaughan for five years) decided to take time off from his gig with Santana, Ed Adair was drafted as the new gear guru. "The day I came onboard," says Adair, "René told me, 'Here, I'm handing you the keys to the Cadillac.' He was right—this is the best ride."

According to Adair, Santana brings four signature Paul Reed Smith guitars on the road—including the original prototype—and strings his namesake PRS models with D'Addario lights, gauged .009–.042. Onstage, Santana plays through two amps: his faithful '72 Mesa Boogie Mk I combo (loaded with a 417 Altec 12") and a 100-watt Dumble head. The Dumble powers a Marshall 4x12 with stock Celestions, and a straight-front 4x12 made by A Brown Soun of San Rafael, California. The Brown Soun cab is loaded with alnico Tone Tubby 12s sporting hemp-paper cones.

"The Brown Soun cab is rather compact, so we use the Marshall to kick out extra bottom," reveals Adair.

For his lively Spanish tones, Santana flatpicks Alvarez classical guitars with factory undersaddle transducers, and, for wah sounds, he uses an ancient Mu-Tron III pedal. Santana wires his rig with Belden 1192A cable.

Royer ribbon mics are a recent addition to Santana's studio rig.

"The combination of the Dumble amp, the hemp speakers, and this new mic means I don't have to look for tone anymore," says Santana. "You just plug in and go 'mamma mia'—even if you're not Italian."

"YOU'RE WORKING IN A FIELD OF MYSTICAL RESONANCE, SOUND, AND VIBRATION"

John McLaughlin, Buddy Guy, and, all of a sudden, three notes right at the core are just you. And in those three notes—the way they were placed in time and space and feeling—you have the seed of a song.

I'm not tripping about Carlos. I'm tripping about what is that melody, and what is that mood? Because those moods are what penetrate people deeply. It's like cracking a walnut—you have to get past the shell to get into the heart of it. You can only do that by playing nonstop for an hour-and-a-half or two hours.

Can you tell us about recording with Plácido Domingo? An operatic tenor and a thumping 4x12 cab make a unique blend.

I wanted to transmute opera, symphony, Afro-Cuban beats, and blues into something new. I'm really grateful for Plácido's spirit. Many opera singers don't want to sing in English—only Italian, Spanish, or German. When I asked him if he'd have a problem singing in English, he said, "Of course not." He's 60 years old, but when he hit that microphone from ten feet away, he sounded like two Marshall amplifiers. And he hit those notes at 3:00 in the morning after doing two concerts with a sore throat.

The dictionary defines a shaman as someone who uses magic to heal, or reveal the hidden. How does this relate to your music?

Absoluteness and totality—that's the message of *Shaman*. If you want to start healing yourself, you have to start feeling, because nothing is real to you unless you feel it. There's something about bending a string that gets inside your vitals—your cojones—and works its way to your brain. The next thing you know, you feel like you're worth more than what's in your wallet or bank account. Sometimes people get so intellectual, cute, and clever with music that only they understand it. To me, music shouldn't be such a mystery. It should be something that all humans can say, "Wow, I feel it—you're touching me in a place I haven't been touched before."

As guitarists, we all want to learn how to get so inside the note that time and space disappear. It comes like an orgasm. When you have an orgasm, you don't know if you're Irish, Mexican, Apache, Japanese, Hebrew, or Palestinian. You're in the fullness of a complete Niagara Falls of absolute totality. And that's where I try to take people with my guitar.

9.

"THERE ARE A LOT OF TONES WITHIN MYSELF THAT I CAN FORM SIMPLY BY LOOKING INWARD"

. . . .

by Darrin Fox, June 2005

I'm proof that a musician can coexist with everyone from Wayne Shorter and Kirk Hammett to Plácido Domingo and P.O.D.," exclaims Carlos Santana, as he reclines in his San Rafael, California, headquarters. "I'll even play with Kenny G., Billy Joel, or Elton John if the song is right."

If that previous quote doesn't confirm that Santana is sticking with the star-infused collaborations that have garnered him tons of mainstream cheese, two smash albums (*Supernatural* and *Shaman*), and an attic's worth of Grammys, well, consider Carlos jamming with Antonio Banderas on the 2005 Academy Awards telecast.

"I thought the whole experience was going to be a lot weirder than it actually was," says Santana. "But after you play Woodstock on acid, nothing's a big deal anymore!"

With the same peaceful strength that stands behind every note he plays, Santana makes it clear that he doesn't care what people think of his star-struck pop collaborations—the latest of which is *All That I Am*.

"I'm not going to have the opportunity to play with Herbie Hancock, and then worry about the weird expectations people put on me, and not work with a talented songwriter like Rob Thomas," he exclaims. "I don't care what people say about Santana playing corporate rock, and I never have. It's like, 'Whatever, man, I'm going to go hang out with Buddy Guy and John Lee Hooker [*laughs*].'" And I've got news for all of those intellectual snobs and brainiacs: You try and write a song like Green Day, and get it on the radio and connect with people. Even John Coltrane connected with larger audiences with 'My Favorite Things'—a pop song. No matter what you're playing, it all comes down to one basic thing: Can you connect with the people—whether it's a three-year old, a 17-year-old, or a 50-year-old? What's the point of speaking an elite musical language that only you can understand?"

It's tough to argue with that—especially when Santana is far more than "just" a popular artist. Sure, his guitar solos are on nearly every radio station across the land, but he has also been an adored and respected collaborator with the likes of John Lee Hooker, Wayne Shorter, and John McLaughlin. And his current workload includes several decidedly non-pop-star projects, such as finishing some tracks with blues legend Buddy Guy, readying the release of the *Santana/Shorter at Montreux* DVD (a performance at 1988's Montreux Jazz Festival), and wrapping up an all-instrumental Santana album. If the preview I heard is any indication, the instrumental record will delight fans of Santana's pure 6-string magic with everything from thoughtful nylon-string workouts ("Gabor") to heavy Latin-rock numbers ("Nomad").

"At this stage of my life, all is one in my eyes," he says. "I don't have to be just the 'Latin rock guy.' If I have the chance, I want to be able to play the Grand Ole Opry, or in the middle of Africa. Look, it's not like I want to be liked by everybody, but who wouldn't want to reach as many people's hearts as they can?"

There aren't many rock guitarists who keep company with people such as Wayne Shorter, John McLaughlin, and John Lee Hooker. Why do you think these players are so accepting of you?

Well, I remember Wynton Marsalis saying that I shouldn't even be on the same stage with Wayne Shorter because I was playing rock music. But Wayne's response was beautiful. He said, "Wynton, you could put children from different parts of the world in the same sandbox, and even though they won't speak the same language, they're still going to play with the same bucket and the same shovel."

But, first and foremost, I think people like Wayne and John Lee read my intentions. They saw it in my eyes that I wasn't there to steal from them or disrespect their music. I'm there to learn from them and honor the music. And that attitude gave me a first-class ticket with those guys.

What's your first reaction when you hear guitarists who have been influenced by your approach to tone and phrasing, such as Los Lonely Boys' Henry Garza or Orianthi?

I cheer so loud, man. It feels good, because for a long time I wasn't sure if people thought of me as an influential guitar player. As a matter of fact, it wasn't until Prince told me that I was a major influence on his playing that I realized maybe I had left a mark with my guitar.

When you recorded *Shaman*, you were over the moon about discovering Dumble amplifiers. Did you have any tonal discoveries on the new albums?

What I'm learning more and more is that there are a lot of tones within myself that I can form simply by looking inward. Sure, Dumbles are incredible amps. But Alexander Dumble himself would tell you that Larry Carlton, Robben Ford, Eric Johnson, and myself have our own fingerprints with or without a Dumble amplifier. I can tell you every little piece of gear I've ever used, and you're still not going to sound like me. Your sound as an individual comes from sitting and playing for one, two, or three hours nonstop. It's where you get into this zone, and something takes over where the music truly plays you, and your mind is free of insecurities. The muscle memory and mechanics will handle themselves at a certain point, and you can get down to the matter of true expression that goes straight to the instrument from your heart. You have to reach inside yourself. There's absolutely no substitute for locking yourself away and not coming out until you have your own sound.

Do you think guitar magazines perpetuate gear lust too much?

Guitar mags have a valid role. They turn people on to the gear that's out there, and help them understand that certain gear sounds a certain way. For example, a Strat is going to sound the way it sounds simply because of its construction. That hasn't changed since Ritchie Valens and Buddy Holly. And with a certain amp, your tone is going to be a certain way.

But people should try to go deeper into the instrument, and transcend its actual construction. To do that, you have to make ugly faces, pucker up your butt, and get to that note. You need to put different levels of brutal freakin' force behind your playing. The next thing you know, you start getting into the territory that Stevie Ray Vaughan and Jeff Beck inhabit. Let's face it, Stevie made some pretty ugly faces. And, hopefully, so do I. Anybody who goes for the note makes that face. It's like having an orgasm. I don't know anybody who looks nice when they have an

ALL THAT GEAR

"For the most part, Carlos' setup has stayed the same," says René Martinez, who, along with Ed Adair, watches after Santana's tonal arsenal. "His main guitar is a stock, green PRS Santana model which he has used consistently for the past year. From his guitar, the signal goes to a switcher box that allows Carlos to choose between two Dumble Overdrive Reverbs and a mid-'70s Mesa/Boogie Mark I head. The Boogie and one Dumble are dialed in with a fair amount of overdrive for sustain, whereas I try to dial in the other Dumble for a cleaner tone. All of the amplifiers are ready to go when Carlos steps onstage, and it's up to him to decide what he wants to hear. Sometimes, he'll only use the Boogie for most of the night, or he'll use all three amps at once. The only effects Carlos uses are a Dunlop 535Q wah and a delay pedal." (Martinez was reluctant to divulge the brand of delay, as Santana is always changing it, but word is he's currently stomping on a T-Rex Replica at rehearsals.)

As for speaker cabs, the Mesa/Boogie Mark I runs into a 1x12 cabinet loaded with a JBL E120 that has been outfitted with a hemp cone for its slightly mellower tone and added durability. The first Dumble Overdrive Special powers two Marshall 4x12 slant cabinets. One is loaded with Celestion Vintage 30s, and the other sports two Vintage 30s and two Celestion G12M-25 greenbacks. The second Dumble drives an A Brown Soun 4x12 open-back cabinet loaded with Tone Tubby 12s.

"Carlos records with this exact stage setup," says Adair, who assisted Santana at Berkeley's Fantasy Studios while the guitarist was recording his two new records. "The only difference being, instead of a delay pedal, we'll use an old 1/4" Studer tape machine or a Lexicon PCM-80 for about 350ms of delay. Carlos tracks everything in the control room, and we typically use Royer ribbon mics on the 4x12s, and a Neumann on the Mesa/Boogie 1x12."

orgasm. And if you're not having an orgasm, then you're not all the way into it like you're supposed to be.

Is there a guitarist who best typifies overcoming an instrument's construction?

Jimi did it. He willed a Strat to do what he wanted it to do. Back then, Strats sounded like the Beach Boys and Jan and Dean and Dick Dale. Not until Jimi came along did the Stratocaster get away from the surf sound. Why do you think Jimi said, "You'll never hear surf music again"? It's not that his music is better or worse than surf, it's just that Jimi wanted a Strat to sound like Mt. St. Helens, so he made it happen.

"The three Bs— Butterfield, Bloomfield, and Bishop were scary, man! They opened up the entire spectrum."

At a certain point, it becomes a question of dedication.

Exactly. Take John Coltrane. He played nonstop—even to the point of going to the kitchen and playing when other guys were soloing on the bandstand! That's supreme dedication. If you go for supreme dedication, you get a bonus—the big tone. But for people who have that kind of dedication, it's almost like they aren't allowed to have quality tender time with other people, or their kids. I don't want that. I don't need that. I'd rather drive my daughter to school. As much as I love music, it's what I do, it's not who I am.

Did you ever start going the route of supreme dedication at the expense of personal relationships?

Sure. But once I had children, I knew I couldn't b.s. myself. My son and two daughters are more important than anything. I'd rather go back to washing dishes in the Mission district than play music and not take care of them.

Can you point to an album of yours as a watershed moment in your development as a player?

There were two: *Caravanserai* [1972] and *Welcome* [1973]. At that time, I felt my whole existence being pulled toward John Coltrane. I remember going to the record company and telling them, "I know what you want, but I can't give it to you because I don't hear it." I knew I would pay the price by not selling a ton of records, but I didn't care.

You've said that you practice with John Coltrane records, but that you don't play or sound like Coltrane. What specifically are you listening for that can be applied to your own style?

I'm trying to get to that tone that's not merely a result of what gear I'm using. When I listen to Coltrane, I hear children playing and birds singing. I'm not romanticizing—that is actually what I hear. It wasn't always that way. His music used to sound like the equivalent of someone opening a fire hydrant. But because I'm open, I began to understand what he was going for. It's the same thing Jimi Hendrix strove toward—tones that serve to remind us that we're multi-dimensional spirits, not just blacks or whites, Jews or Mexicans. That's small stuff.

Are there any guitarists who you go to for that kind of inspiration?

I still find myself going back to my John Lee Hooker and Jimmy Reed albums. I just read a Branford Marsalis interview where he said that he noticed his tone improved when he started listening to more John Lee Hooker and Son House. Something about their music compels you to look at the bigger picture of tone—not just a guitar or an amplifier. You'd be surprised how much time I spend with the Paul Butterfield Blues Band's *East-West*, too. That album was a major groundbreaker. The three Bs—Butterfield, Bloomfield, and Bishop were scary, man! They opened up the entire spectrum.

How much do you feel a person's life experiences add to their depth as a player?

Well, there's the saying, "To get to it, you gotta go through it." But the flip side of that was Miles Davis, who said, "My dad is rich. My mom is good looking. I've never suffered, nor do I intend to suffer. But, man, I can play some blues." So he broke that stereotype. It's funny—I remember John Lee Hooker telling me that a lot of people play the blues, but if they don't wear those silky pimp socks, he doesn't believe them [*laughs*]. As for me, I knew when I saw B. B. King for the first time, I had to leave my mom and move out with no one to wash my clothes and cook for me. It wasn't that I was looking to suffer. I just knew that I had to go out and get some real, first-hand life experience in order to create.

"THERE ARE A LOT OF TONES WITHIN MYSELF THAT I CAN FORM SIMPLY BY LOOKING INWARD"

Do you ever look at your fabulous success and think about the players you came up with—say Elvin Bishop or Harvey Mandel or Mike Bloomfield—and ask, "Why me?"

Of course. I remember standing onstage accepting a Grammy from Bob Dylan and Lauryn Hill, and I swear, guys like Tommy Castro and Otis Rush were going through my mind, and all I could think about was, "Why me?" And then, all of a sudden, I hear this voice that says, "Because of your heart." See, my heart wants to wake people up to their full potential. And to realize that potential in yourself, your heart must dictate to your brain. It should never be the other way around. If your brain dictates to your heart, then you're just shucking and jiving. No person or thing is going to validate you more than your own heart. So which one do you want to hang with?

10.

"EGO ONLY HAS ONE AGENDA—TO CREATE DEATH, DESTRUCTION, AND FAILURE"

by Michael Molenda, December 2008

In addition to being a great friend to *Guitar Player* over the years, Carlos Santana has endeavored to fire up the magazine's creative juices by hipping the staff to noteworthy under-the-radar guitarists, as well as sending us mix CDs full of music that has inspired him. Every few months, I'll receive a little package from his San Rafael, California, offices bearing something delightful, inspirational, or out-and-out humbling. It's kind of a one-way relationship, however, as Santana is so in tune with what's going on in every musical universe that it seems hopeless I would ever come across an artist, style, or technique that would surprise him. (I don't think my quest for the perfectly distorted punk-rock *A* chord qualifies as a "discovery of note.") Furthermore, his adventurous and inquisitive spirit leads him to consider much more about what it means to be a guitarist than one's choice of a favored style and the gear needed to construct a suitable tone.

So it wasn't really a surprise when Santana artfully dodged a discussion of his gear and tonal evolution in the wake of his new, dual-CD compilation, *Multi-Dimensional Warrior*—a handpicked collection of vocal songs and instrumentals spanning nearly four decades of the guitarist's prodigious musical output.

"I'd like to talk about intangibles," he said when first contacted about this cover story. "I haven't changed my gear all that much since the last

Guitar Player story [June '05], and I'd like to get beyond those physical things and think about the roles of the heart and mind in making music."

Santana was so excited about the concept that he proceeded to suggest several more article ideas, a few twists on the typical guitar book and lesson DVDs, and, I think, even a live-concert event. (It was a bit hard to keep up with the snappy tempo of his well-considered proposals.) And, trust me, when Carlos Santana is that thrilled about a subject, you go with it. So what follows is a bit of a different *Guitar Player* article, but one that is no less instructive or valuable than a treatise on tone and technique. Few artists in these pages have attempted to detail the messy and often inexplicable engines of imagination, inspiration, and creation. (The last time was likely Bill Nelson's "Chasing the Muse" feature in the March '04 issue.) By necessity, the discussion tends to leave the world of the pragmatic, and sails into areas that can be uncomfortable for many players—God, spirituality, openness, self-assessment, self-awareness, ego, habit, ambition, and the potential evil of comfort zones. But if a player seeks to truly jettison stylistic mimicry, and fight like a cornered jackal to develop a unique and personal musical fingerprint, then studying the creative ramifications of intangibles is an essential part of the mission. In this quest, you couldn't have a better guide and confidant than Carlos Santana.

What directed your selection of the songs on *Multi-Dimensional Warrior?*

What happened was that I had just come home from Hawaii, where I realized how Bob Marley's music was made. It's all from the islands and the clouds and the waves. It's very calm and peaceful and pure, and you can just focus on nothing—which is very difficult for the ego to do, because the ego has "ifs" and "buts" firing off all the time. And while I was not thinking about anything, I heard a voice say, "Carlos, go to your cassettes, records, and CDs, and compile a letter to your fans." I found myself drawn to music that didn't get heard anywhere near as much as *Abraxas* or *Supernatural*, as well as the desire to turn people on to freedom and the light within themselves—like Bob Marley and John Coltrane. Everything just came so naturally that it was like composing a love letter.

"EGO ONLY HAS ONE AGENDA—TO CREATE DEATH, DESTRUCTION, AND FAILURE"

Some musicians might consider a "letter to their fans" to be a greatest hits package, but as you consciously avoided that approach, what does this collection represent for you?

Thank you for asking that. There's a part of me that loves learning from musicians such as John Lee Hooker, Jimmy Reed, B. B. King, and Miles Davis. But there's also a part of me that wants to invest—like Desmond Tutu or the Dalai Lama or Harry Belafonte—in the healing of the common man. So it's not enough for me to play music, learn from all these guys, and be recognized worldwide. I also want to serve—to be of service. We are capable of creating miracles ourselves, and the greatest miracle is to create a masterpiece of joy out of your life with no excuses. This is what led to the combination of songs on *Multi-Dimensional Warrior*—I wanted people to taste their own triumph through this music. In fact, I was amazed how many times the word "light" appears in all the songs with lyrics.

So I'm assuming the album title isn't just a clever turn of phrase?

Oh, no [*laughs*]. When people have asked me to define "multi-dimensional," I say that it's not being stuck or stuck up. When you start thinking that you're superior or inferior—that's being stuck. Your fear has betrayed you. Being free is seeing the beauty of you in everybody else. You say, "I can see myself in this guy and that guy. I want to phrase like Otis Redding and Nat King Cole and Wes Montgomery." You see the connections between what you do and what all the musicians before you have done, and between what every musician is doing right now. So I'm grateful that your magazine is here, because you remind people that we're all in it together. *Guitar Player* is multi-dimensional.

Could you elaborate on what you mean by saying "your fear has betrayed you"?

Fear only has one agenda—to negate your beauty and your truth. Ego only has one agenda—to create death, destruction, and failure. That's the only function of the ego. We should compliment it, because at least it's predictable. E-g-o stands for "Etch God Out." But even an atheist can understand the need for wonderment. You don't have to believe in God. God believes in you. God could not care less if you call him Buddha, Allah, Jesus, or Krishna. The best part of you—that's what God is, and it is in all of us. It's called the spark of the divine.

Rays of Light: Santana soloing at Fiddler's Green Amphitheater in Denver, Colorado, September 13, 2008. (© SCOTT D. SMITH / RETNA LTD.)

"EGO ONLY HAS ONE AGENDA—TO CREATE DEATH, DESTRUCTION, AND FAILURE"

Do you remember that scene in *2001: A Space Odyssey* where the astronaut was being bombarded with all these colors? It's like some type of Coltrane solo, or Jimi when he's feeding back. That's what we call the stream of consciousness—which is actually the state of grace, because all is one and one is all. The mind is not equipped to understand that, because the mind likes to compartmentalize. The heart just takes it all in.

But how does a musician transcend compartmentalization? In many ways, we are driven to embrace specific styles such as rock or jazz or blues—which are large compartments—and then there are mini compartments such as scales, chords, and riffs.

The thing I focus on—whether I'm playing with Kirk Hammett or John McLaughlin—is going straight to the heart. I go to mine first, because if I don't feel it, you're not going to feel it. I take a deep breath, and I remind myself that before I give it to you, I have to give it to myself. I have to receive it. It doesn't matter if I drink a shot of tequila, or half a glass of wine, or if I smoke a toke, or if I'm totally straight and just drinking water—none of that is going to get in my way. We are talking about intangibles now. The intangible is that thing you put your finger in, and it's wet and it gives you chills. It's half of the equation. It's not just the amplifier or the string. It's not Fender. It's not Gibson. It's not your technique, or Dorian scales, or even chords. When I am open to the intangibles, I can play with Buddy Guy and hold my own, because Buddy Guy is a hurricane, and if you're not playing from your heart, he will wash you out.

Although musicians talk about it a lot, I think the role of the heart in actual creative performance remains a huge mystery. A guitarist can more clearly understand technique. He or she can say, "Buddy Guy is over there, and I've practiced this blues scale forever. I can fly over the notes, add a few tricks, and not give any ground. I'm going to burn."

That's not going to help you. I've seen Buddy destroy a couple of musicians. I won't say their names, because I don't want to hurt their feelings. But they were playing a gazillion notes per second, while he was holding one note, and he looked like a man who was on top of the Grand Canyon wielding a lightning bolt that sounded like Jimi Hendrix. He's holding that one note, and he's grinning at these guys playing a bunch of little notes that sound like mosquitoes stuck in a screen door. That's not going to hurt him. But he'll hurt you with one note that transcends the blues, and all the equipment he's using. That's heart, and Buddy Guy has an incredible heart.

Well, once again, that's fabulous for Buddy Guy, but how can someone who has been taught to trust the rewards of practicing gestures best understand the implications of following their heart?

Everyone has a heart, of course, so it typically comes down to how much you are willing to let it come out. How fast can you get to your heart and not let anything get in the way—children, the rent, the set list, taxes, nothing? How fast can you get to that place in your heart where you don't even have to think about what to play, because the notes will play themselves? Those are the best notes. Listen, carrying a melody is very difficult for a musician, because in order to carry a melody, you have to let go. A lot of people carry chords and speed. Let them go. Let go of everything you have learned, and, in return, receive the thing that will be channeled through you. Don't the best articles you've written just appear? And you go, "Wow, I don't even know how I put those words together!" This is the center of it. Musicians hear 1,000 voices saying they're not good enough—that they're just lucky, that they always play out of tune or their tone sucks, that they never get it right. John Lennon once said he hated everything he did, because he could have done it better. That's the ego. All those voices are the ego in disguise giving you guilt, shame, judgment, condemnation, and fear that you're never going to be good enough. Then you have one voice that is very quiet, but it's louder and clearer than the other voices. This voice says, "Pick up the guitar. Here it comes." And out comes a song that's like Jeff Beck playing "People Get Ready" [sings the main melody]. Bam! Your freaking hair stands up, you've got tears coming out of your eyes, and you don't even know why. These are the things that drive me to go inside my heart, and going there is the only thing that is worth attaining for me. When I'm there, the heart will lead me to play a melody that makes families put all their sh*t aside, and just see how beautiful their families are. That's what is really beautiful about music—it brings you into harmony. The other stuff you can learn by repetition, like a hamster. With willingness, you can truly learn why people adore Jimi Hendrix.

"EGO ONLY HAS ONE AGENDA—TO CREATE DEATH, DESTRUCTION, AND FAILURE"

Can you be a bit more specific about the role of willingness?

Let's look at it this way—what is this intangible world that Jimi Hendrix and Beethoven dipped into? You can call it hocus- pocus or whatever, but this world exists. How often are you willing to dip into it? Do you dip into it at all? Do you ever have those moments where you're playing by yourself, and you think you've been at it for 30 minutes, but you suddenly realize you've got sweat and saliva all over your guitar because you've been at it for more than two hours? I think this is the next step for *Guitar Player* magazine. You should invite people to go beyond the mechanics of the physical brain and the fingers, and go to that place where—like one of my favorite bands, the Doors—we can all open the doors to perception. When you hear Robby Krieger's creepy minor-major blues thing at the beginning of "The End," it's like Dracula giving you a hug, but you don't mind it. I love music that makes me feel like I'm seven years old, going to the movies for the first time and experiencing Panavision. That's why we love Jimi Hendrix—he assaults all of our senses. His music has a wide circumference. Hendrix is another name for a bridge to the unknown, because what he was playing, even he couldn't reproduce sometimes. He couldn't quantize it—as much as he might have tried to get back there by taking seven tabs of acid and a little bit of wine and some coke. Sometimes, it's nothing—just the willingness. The willingness to take a deep breath and take what was given to you. It's inside you, as John Lee Hooker said, and it has to come out. But maybe you won't let it out, because you want to analyze it before it comes out. Don't analyze it. Leave that for other people. Just take a deep breath, stop what you're thinking, and let go. Let God light you up, and let it come out. Then you can get rid of all the sh*t you know, and play things that sound like singing water.

Intangibles and willingness are, by definition, far more mysterious than pragmatic results—such as mastering a difficult melodic run. The poet William Blake was a visionary who spoke to angels, Jackson Pollack was a drunk, and Jimi Hendrix took drugs. Those are just three examples of artists swimming in pure creative inspiration. While I'd never advocate the abuse of alcohol or pharmaceuticals, is there some trigger needed to launch a musician beyond the concrete and into the unknown?

I don't need to take acid or mescaline to trip anymore, but I learned enough from that stuff to realize what Einstein meant when he said, "Imagination is more important than knowledge." Your imagination is your best equipment, and you cannot learn it or earn it—it was given to you. Take it. It's yours. You don't have to go down to the crossroads, and wait for a black cat or the full moon. You don't have to sell yourself to the devil. What for? You have God's love, and what can be better than that? Whether you're Yngwie Malmsteen or Steve Vai or Joe Satriani or John Scofield, you just need to shut everything off and utilize the main television—your imagination.

You see, the ultimate destination for guitar players is to create heaven and wonderment for both themselves and the listeners. If you're not doing that, you're just shucking and jiving. But if you can let go and trust God, then you can change yourself, and then you can change me, and we can change everybody. What is deep inside of you is something that might make Buddy Guy turn around and say, "Hmmm—that's interesting." And then everyone else starts saying, "Damn, did you hear this new cat? He has a very fertile imagination."

Here's another way of looking at it. I loved the debate in your letters column [September '08] commenting on Al Di Meola and Kenny Neal [who were both profiled in the July '08 *GP*] talking separately about whether it's better to express yourself with one note or one million notes. But let's suppose that you can express a million things with one note. Let's consider for a moment that it's not wishful thinking, or a lazy man's way of justifying not practicing. How would you go about doing it? Is it the amplifier? Is it your technique? Is it the guitar? Do you need sympathetic strings like Ravi Shankar? Or can you use your imagination to see a note as a crystal that you put next to the sun, and that crystal then reflects the whole spectrum of the rainbow. Now, you can play for half an hour in each color! Your imagination is what makes this possible. You just have to invite your imagination into your creative process.

Now, let me comment a little bit on the pragmatic or tangible aspects of playing guitar that you've been mentioning. To me, getting all the scales and gear together is like practicing in a mirror while sucking in your cheeks. You're posing. Don't let the scales and the speed and the knowledge of chords and gear get in the way of that note that's going to

"EGO ONLY HAS ONE AGENDA—TO CREATE DEATH, DESTRUCTION, AND FAILURE"

disarm other people's egos and make every hair on their body stand up. Then they get to a place where they say to you, "You know, Michael, that note touched me in a place I've never been touched before." All of a sudden, your playing is not about comparing or competing. You go to a place where you become like what Derek Trucks is to me—a minister. In your ministry, you utilize music to take people back to where they have always been, and to where they have never been. You want to play a note that's so beautiful that the audience goes [*makes gasping noise*], and they can't breathe out until you finish your phrase.

Do you know Sonny Sharrock? He could shred like a tornado—like the Tasmanian Devil—and then create melodies out of all that madness. When people smoke cigars while they're playing cards, and the smoke goes to the ceiling and creates something beautiful—that's Sonny Sharrock. He is the person I wish was still alive more than any other musician, because I think he was in between Jimi Hendrix and Coltrane more than anybody.

Actually, Sharrock taught me about savvy repetition. I forgot the name of his song, but I played it constantly because it held onto a theme seemingly forever, but it was never boring. In fact, it was quite beguiling, and I drove myself nuts trying to deconstruct what Sonny was doing to make something that should have been mind-numbingly tedious so evocative and musical.

It's a good thing you brought that up, because I think people need to understand that there's a difference between repetition and a spell. A spell is another word for wonderment. No matter who you are, that's what you long to get into. Otherwise, you're going to get bored with your sh*t. But you will never be bored with your wonderment. Wonderment has nothing to do with scales or repetition or amplifiers. It has to do with your own being, and what's inside your heart. Your mind will just be like, "Okay, I can't quantize this or understand it, so I'll just shut up and be quiet." Behold—that's wonderment.

You know, being from San Francisco, like you, we have something over the rest of this nation. I don't consider San Franciscans inferior or superior, but we do have an edge because we dare to think outside the box—musically, politically, aesthetically, and philosophically. We get accused of—"Oh yeah, that reminds me of the cows and the cheese. You know how the California people are." But, the fact is, we invest time and energy pursuing the intangible. That's the vortex we're talking about—that state of grace where you go beyond what you know and the equipment you're using. You get into that place where everybody in your band is looking at you, and they're going, "Damn! What the hell was that?"

Here's a recent example of what I'm talking about. I played a benefit concert last year for Angela Bofill with [drummer] Narada Michael Walden and [keyboardist] Chester Thompson at Grace Cathedral in San Francisco, and, as I was waiting for my solo, a voice said to me, "Carlos, this is the Grace Cathedral, and people are used to hearing 'Ave Maria,' but I want you to go to this Sonny Sharrock/Coltrane place and bug out. You're going to show people and yourself that the halo and the horns are cool. Go for it." But, just then, I looked at Chester and he was gone. His eyes were closed, and he was giving it his all. I looked at Narada, and he was gone, too. He looked like a cross-eyed lion. And I realized, "Man, they're there already. I have to go to another place. Can I do it?" So I changed my stance, and I went for it. I said, "I'm going for it, and if I get a freaking heart attack, then I die. I don't care." A month later, people who saw the concert were still telling me, "You created this vortex between heaven and earth that I know wasn't of this planet." I said, "I know exactly when I went for it, and I'm glad you picked up on it." You see, people intuitively applaud your pursuance—not necessarily the attainment. For example, you can perform a perfect solo, and the people might say, "Eh, whatever," because maybe you were 99 percent perfect, but you were an asshole about reaching that final one percent of perfection. You weren't open and giving, and your ego was too involved, so people will only remember that you were an asshole. The true beauty is in the pursuance, so I'd recommend looking at that one percent "shortfall" as the sacrifice you had to make in order for the other notes to be perfect. It's funny, Wayne Shorter once said, "I like mistakes. Sometimes, big ones—like scars."

That's interesting. I just interviewed Alvin Lee from Ten Years After about how the British Invasion players took American blues and revved it up into the blues-rock hybrid. He said that, back then, they didn't really have a lot of influences to relate to, and that many of the blues solos they heard were far from perfect. There were

"EGO ONLY HAS ONE AGENDA—TO CREATE DEATH, DESTRUCTION, AND FAILURE"

tons of mistakes. So what he and his peers got from the original blues guitarists was their energy and passion—which is why he said he still cranks up his amp and goes for feel over precision to this day. The whole thing about striving for so-called "perfect" rock solos came later.

Here's where we crystallize this statement—for you, for me, and for everybody. Perfect perfection exists in the heart, not in the mind. Perfect perfection is—I just learned this word, man, and I want to share it with you—"unalterable." It means something that you can't add to, because it's already perfect. People say, "What's that?" The sun. The sun has never said to the earth, "You owe me," so it's unalterable. The Mona Lisa is unalterable. You can't add anything to it, or subtract anything from it. The eyes of a brand new baby are unalterable. Within those eyes is pure innocence, and they are incapable of disappointing you. I think it's good news to understand that perfect perfection does exist, but there are certain things musicians need to identify in order for them to play music that uplifts, transforms, and moves people beyond show business—beyond "look what I can do"—and to a place where people drop their guard and go, "Wow!"

A lot of people practice everything meticulously, and they go onstage and play it meticulously exactly the same way. Now, this can be incredible, but, after a while, it's like watching something through plexiglass—you can't get to the other side. Me—I need a hug. I don't kiss the air like the kids in Los Angeles. Give me a hug. So I feel that people really need to learn how to hug that note.

How do you "hug" a note?

Well, I was recording this supreme singer once, and he said, "Carlos, I'm inside this vocal booth, and you're out there in the control room, so tell me where I am." Now, whether it's Pavarotti or Larry Graham, I always say the same thing: "You're going around the block. Get inside the sheets." That means to get a little closer to the melody. And don't make it staccato—make it legato. Legato is a hug. That's why we love Peter Green—"The Supernatural" is all legato.

So you're not down with staccato phrasing—like, say, how a horn section might place its accents?

Oh, there's also a need for staccato. It's fun. It's like skipping rocks across a lake. "Ch-ch-ch-ch-splash." Hey, can you skip it seven times?

Let's talk a bit about leading a band. When I saw you perform at the Fillmore in San Francisco last month, I was amazed at how much your band members were listening to everything going on around them. It seemed you never had to cue them—you'd change a feel, and they'd just adapt immediately, as if everyone was psychic. These moments didn't seem rehearsed or choreographed—they'd just happen. How do you ensure every player is on the same wavelength?

Thank you for saying that. My answer to your question is "trust." My band members trust me. The only things I ever rehearse are grooves. I want to make sure you put your finger in it, and you touch it with your tongue, and it's freaking divinely delicious. The tempo has to be right for a certain song. We can't fall in different places. It's just like football—there can't be no penalty flags! We all have to hit the collective "wa."

SANTANA'S LOVE LETTER

"When I started picking out songs, the process just flew, and I didn't hesitate over anything or second-guess any of my choices," says Santana of his personal selection and sequencing of the tracks on *Multi-Dimensional Warrior*. "Everything just felt right. It was like writing a love letter."

The 28-track, dual-CD release is a welcome left turn from the typical repackaging practices of many labels. For one thing, there's the obvious fact that Santana himself was intimately involved in the project—even to the point of supervising the recording of brand new parts for a few songs. He added guitars to "Spirit" and "Right Now," had Chester Thompson lay down a piano on "Let There Be Light," and directed Barbara Higbie to track harp melodies for "Praise" and "Let There Be Light."

Perhaps most importantly, however, Santana abandoned the (re)hawk-the-hits tactic in favor of presenting an uplifting and undulating soundscape of moods, vibes, and rhythmic feels from the past 30-plus years of his oeuvre. As a result, Multi-Dimensional Warrior lives up to its title, unfolding as a harmonious symphony of themes, rather than a disconnected collection of songs. It's also one of those rare occasions where we get a peek into an artist's re-evaluation of his or her music, guided and nurtured only by the experiences and wisdom they've sustained over the passing years, and uncorrupted by purely commercial considerations. Oh yeah, and the guitar playing totally rocks.

"EGO ONLY HAS ONE AGENDA—TO CREATE DEATH, DESTRUCTION, AND FAILURE"

You should do an article in *Guitar Player* on wa. What the hell is the wa? Imagine 100 women in a circle around you in the middle of a field, and they're all going, "Hey ya, nay nay , , , wa!" When you all hit the wa together—that's when music is happening. So I tell my band, "I need the wa. Let's hit the wa together. Don't overstate it, but visit it." All music, whether it's Segovia or Paco de Lucia or Hendrix, has the wa. If you don't hit the wa, your music is redundant, repetitious, and monotonous. James Brown called it "hitting on the one," and he visited the wa enough to put a collective conscious on it. A lot of bands have come from James Brown.

Do you listen for melodic clues from drummers?

Absolutely. Tony Williams, Elvin Jones, Mitch Mitchell, Ginger Baker—these are drummers who know how to be possessed, and, as a result, they can take the guitar player beyond what he can play. Drummers play melodies in the cymbals, and if you hear them—whether you're Pat Metheny or John Scofield—it's like, "Man, you played something in the cymbals that brought me to a whole other room in the house I haven't visited before."

Again, we're talking about being open and trusting yourself to finding inspiration in everything around you.

My Uncle Max used to say, "By any means necessary." So show me the brilliance. Show me the wonderment. Don't show me excuses. No ifs, no buts, no slipping, no sliding, no superiority, no inferiority. Don't let what you know get in the way. Get to that place where everyone is uplifted in spirit and revived.

Unfortunately, there's a fair amount of pressure on ambitious young musicians to clone what's successful, as many of today's besieged record labels are practicing strict "risk management." Do you feel you can embrace the spirit and still serve commerce?

The more McDonald's that are out there, the more you need a grand-ma who spends all day in the kitchen stirring the sauce on Thanksgiving. This is why I'm very grateful to Derek Trucks, Ben Harper, Trey Anastasio, and others like them. They are successful, and they play from their hearts. Now, there are a lot of successful posers, as well. These are the musicians I was talking about who practice in front of mirrors, and plan every note to do a certain thing. It's all calculated. But I think these people would be afraid to get onstage with Jeff Beck,

Buddy Guy, and me, because they would think they'd have to compete with Jeff Beck, Buddy Guy, and me. I don't compete or compare, man. I just wait my turn.

Can we explore that a bit? You've shared stages with a lot of amazing guitarists and other instrumentalists. How do you approach your performance when you're sharing licks with another player?

If they go up and down, I go from side to side. I'm going to bring counter motion to whatever is happening in the room. I figure the best way I can be welcome is to bring something different from what they're doing. That's what I learned from Miles Davis: Always go for the counter motion. It's a great insight. He said, "If you hear something, don't play it. Play what's around it. Play like you don't know what to play." Again, this is about letting go of what you know.

I'm still a bit of a coward. If I'm hearing *A*, *C#m*, *F#m*, *D*, I'm probably going to surrender to my comfort zone and play an *A* major scale.

Here's that word again: Trust. In order to trust, you have to be able to see something beautiful first, and then feel something beautiful. I can close my eyes, and in this very second I can be Buddy Guy, John McLaughlin, Pat Metheny, and Jeff Beck, and we're all having a ball. We don't even know we're guitar players. We're just saying, "Hey man," and each one of us is telling some marvelous stories. Buddy has some great blues stories about Muddy Waters and B. B. King and John Lee Hooker. So tell me a story with your guitar, man. If I wanted to see a screwdriver or a hammer, I'd ask you to play me scales and chords. You see what I mean? You have to learn how to tell a story. You have to learn to carry a melody. You have to learn to access the intangible at will. These things will make you a different kind of musician.

Ultimately, you should utilize music the same way you utilize your imagination. Sometimes, you can just drop something in and make people go, "Wow!" It doesn't have to be deep. For example, there's a place in our set—between "Soul Sacrifice" and the finale—where the band doesn't know what I'm going to do. I might play something raw or beautiful, or I'll throw in a Looney Tunes theme. Any direction is okay, because music doesn't have to be so boring, constrictive, and serious. Music is supposed to be fun.

LESSONS

11.

CLASSIC CARLOS: A PORTRAIT OF DORIAN UN-GRAY

by Jesse Gress, January 1993

Ever find yourself feeling less than inspired by the latest wave of half-baked, generic music? One sure remedy is immersion in the music of the masters. And who better personifies the ideal of the musician who is emotionally committed to every note than Carlos Santana? When Santana hit the international scene in 1969 with a sound that combined jazz, blues, rock, and Latin, no one had yet coined that notorious "f" word—"fusion."

Carlos' playing sounded totally unlike anything in rock. Abstractly speaking, many of Santana's melodic lines are constructed from the usual materials: pentatonic major and minor scales, blues scales, and diatonic modes (he particularly favors Dorian). But rhythm may be the most important aspect of Carlos' playing. If you were to remove the pitches from his melodic lines, the pure rhythms would be as much at home on a conga or timbale as on the guitar. When working out the following examples, try learning the rhythms before adding the notes. Some aspects of Carlos' playing are difficult to translate on paper. His breathy elastic rhythms often defy accurate notation by accelerating ahead of or dropping slightly behind the beat. One way to get a handle on this "bouncing ball" effect is to practice rhythms in which each successive beat is increased or decreased by evenly divided accent (see **Fig. 1**).

Fig. 1

A typical Santana solo—if there is such a thing—might contain blues-drenched call-and-response phrases, unexpected melodic twists colored with intervals outside of the pedestrian pentatonic scale, syncopated rhythm motifs, a tremolo-picked slow glissando moving to a climactic high bend, and perhaps conclude with an infinitely sustained note. (In the live Osaka version of "Europa," Carlos holds one note for 59 seconds!) And, of course, every note drips with that inexplicable something that the late music critic Ralph J. Gleason once described as the "X-factor." Though we can barely scratch the surface, here are a few of Carlos' finest.

Ex. 1 is one of Santana's most familiar early-period licks. Begin in the tenth position, making sure you milk the release of the first bend for all it's worth. Enhance the heavy Peter Green vibe with a slide into the 9th (*E*); also the 5th of the Vm chord (*Am*).

Ex. 2 begins with a two-bar call-and-response phrase featuring sixteenth-note syncopations. The phrase repeats and then concludes with a dip to the ♭7 (*C*), eventually returning to the tonic *D* via a lazy quarter-note triplet. This flurry of activity followed by a long sustained resolution is another Santana trademark.

Framed by a signature Im–IV Dorian vamp (*Am–D*), **Ex. 3** finds Carlos playing musical question and answer between the upper and middle registers of the fifth-position *A* Dorian mode. The half-step slides into the *F♯*s evoke Wes Montgomery and George Benson.

A combination of ascending bends peppered with dramatic rests and mixed rhythmic groupings creates a sense of urgency in the opening measure of **Ex. 4**. For the shift back to the twelfth position, play the *F♯* at the end of bar 1 with your middle or ring finger so you can comfortably finger the remaining *E* Dorian/pentatonic minor phrase. The underlying chord progression is built from a harmonized *E* pentatonic minor scale.

While **Ex. 5**'s sax-like opening figure is derived from the *F* harmonic minor scale, you can also think of it as a *C7* arpeggio played over the *F* Dorian vamp. Bars 2 and 3 superimpose arpeggiated *E♭*, and *B♭*, major triads, followed by a short B. B. King-ism. Next, two chromatically descending 4ths raise the tension. Barre the 16th fret with your 3rd finger and the 15th with your 2nd finger to assure a comfortable arrival at the thirteenth position for the bluesy wrap-up in bar 5.

CLASSIC CARLOS: A PORTRAIT OF DORIAN UN-GRAY

Ex. 6 exemplifies Carlos' Coltrane-infused collaborations with John McLaughlin. Santana opens with a descending *F♯* pentatonic minor scale superimposed over a *B* Mixolydian vamp (A6–B). Note how these rhythms accelerate, as we discussed earlier. The *D♯* alludes to *F♯* Dorian (relative to *B* Mixolydian, as do the following pair of broken minor-third intervals descending in whole steps. The next minor third descends only a half-step, bringing the ♭5 into the picture for a split second before moving back to *F♯* Dorian. The phrase beginning at the end of bar 4 moves from low-register, twelfth position *F♯* pentatonic minor to a rapid, sixteenth-note ascent via *F♯* Dorian. A tremolo-picked even gliss beginning on F# peaks with a high bend into *C♯*. Extremely hip: the fact that this *C♯* and the notes of the closing *F♯* pentatonic minor lick are the 9, ♭7, and 5 of the tonic *B*.

A lush IV–I progression in *C* (*Fmaj7–Cmaj7*) accompanies **Ex. 7**'s combination of seventh and eighth-position *C* major scale and fifth-position *C* major pentatonic (phrased as *A* pentatonic minor). The final two measures offer proof that you don't have to play a lot of notes if you've got a good sense of rhythm.

Representative of Carlos' current work, **Ex. 8** offers another lively Im-IV D Dorian vamp. Here, in tenth position, he plays a short, memorable rhythm motif, rests for three beats, then plays a perfectly executed sixteenth-note phrase that flows seamlessly into a restatement of the first motif. Note the "mirror image" sixteenth-note groupings on beats 2 and 3 of the second measure. The concluding lick leans heavily on the 6th (*B*), a key Dorian ingredient.

In **Ex. 9**, unison bends on the 9th kick off an *F* Mixolydian excursion combining Carlos' legato stylings and salsa rhythms. After the sustained bends, Santana hammers and pulls his way down the B string to first position. The extra-hot *F* Mixolydian conclusion contains a beautifully placed 9th (*G*) where one might normally expect to hear the root.

Ex. 10 shows a more recent variation of the accelerating rhythm effect, this time using pull-offs. Begin with your 2nd finger (to accommodate the fingering of the final lick) and think "bouncing ball." The unique closing lick combines twelfth position *E* Dorian and blues scales, and it's just one more reason why we love you, Carlos!

III

CLASSIC CARLOS: A PORTRAIT OF DORIAN UN-GRAY

Ex. 6

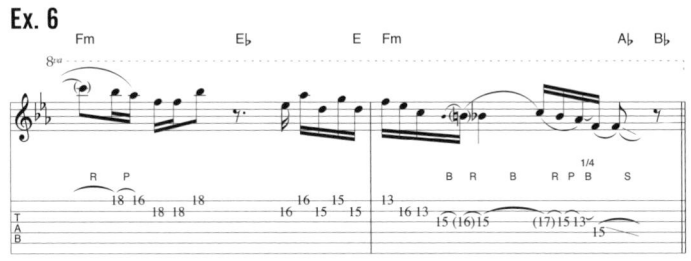

Ex. 7

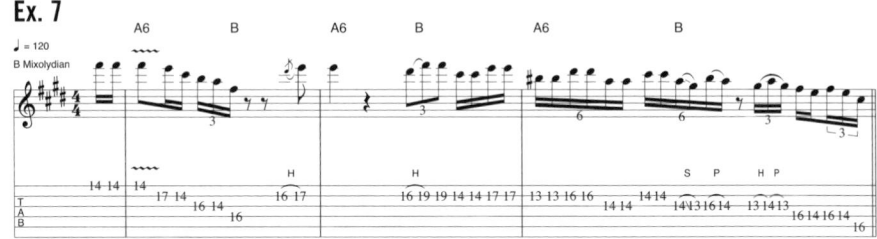

Ex. 8

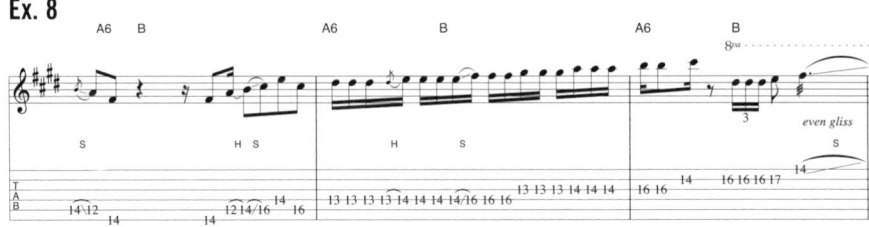

Ex. 9

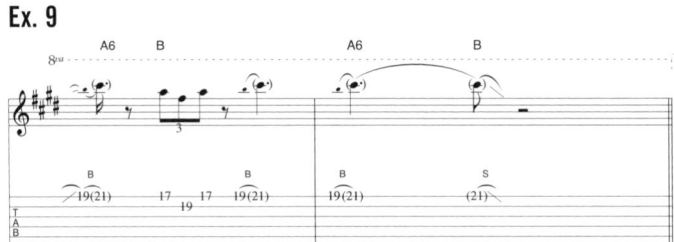

Ex. 10

12.

GUTS AND GRACE: EXPLORE THE TOUGH SENSUALITY OF SANTANA'S LINES

by Andy Ellis, August 1999

It's fun to deconstruct a great guitarist's characteristic phrases. Discovering something as simple as a new fingering or note sequence can alter your perspective of the fretboard and open the door to fresh sounds. Santana puts it best: "We all come from T-Bone Walker, Django Reinhardt, and Charlie Christian, and it shows in our music, man. It's like what [jazz composer] Gil Evans said, 'Take what you need, but honor it.' The kings—Otis Rush, Buddy Guy, Wes Montgomery—we honor all of them. But remember to always make it yours."

Santana's fiery fretwork on "Evil Ways," "Samba Pa Ti," "Black Magic Woman," "Oye Como Va," "Jingo," and "Everybody's Everything" (all found on *Santana—Greatest Hits*), is full of inspiring ideas. Distilled from these early classics, the lines in this lesson are ready for you to honor and make your own.

SYNCOPATION AND SLURS

Ex. 1 is clearly inspired by Peter Green. Emphasize the syncopation (on the and of beat two), and accent the anticipated *E* going into bar 2. Pick close to the bridge,

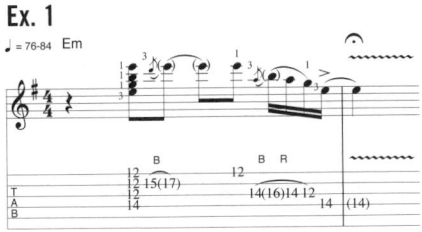

Ex. 1

using a fairly clean tone and a generous dose of reverb. The bend, release, and pull-off (bar 1, beat four) add a vocal quality to the sixteenth notes and keep them from sounding choppy. Santana played this over *Em*, but the lick also works nicely against the IV7 of an *E* blues—*A7* or *A9*.

The first two beats in **Ex. 2** contain one of Santana's favorite moves: a matching pair of triplets played across the top two strings. The whole-step bend and release keeps each triplet smooth. Notice how Examples 1 and 2 end with the identical melodic figure. However, it occurs a beat earlier in **Ex. 2**. Such rhythmic displacement lets you get maximum mileage from any motif.

FILLING THE CRACKS

Ex. 3 borrows several ideas from the previous two examples. Like Ex. 1, this lick starts on beat two. In a band, the bass and drums typically nail the first beat of a given measure, so to avoid competing with the low frequencies of the kick drum and bass, it makes sense to start a melodic phrase after this big downbeat. Santana is a master at working the rhythmic "cracks," and will often launch a lick on a weak beat or on the and of a strong beat.

As in Ex. 2, Santana rolls triplets—each containing a bend and release—across the top strings. This time, there are three bends—two half-step stretches, followed by a whole-step squeeze. The concluding half-step slide takes us from a *Dm* chord tone (*F*) to an *Am* chord tone (*E*). Slick.

In **Ex. 4**, Santana uses hammers and pulls to make a busy line sing instead of chatter. That opening whole-step bend—yeah, way up there at the 18th fret—is a signature Santana exclamation. For an authentic "yow," quickly slide down the string immediately after stretching into high *C*. This sounds great with some reverb. Lean into each hammered *F*—this will help you feel the syncopation.

Ex. 5a reveals Santana's jazzy side. Played over *Gm*—the IVm in a *D* minor blues—it emphasizes the 9 (*A*). This lick lies nicely on the fretboard and sounds just as cool an octave lower (**Ex. 5b**). In either case, keep beat one crisp by accenting the first A and snapping the hammer and pull.

GUTS AND GRACE: EXPLORE THE TOUGH SENSUALITY
OF SANTANA'S LINES

Ex. 2

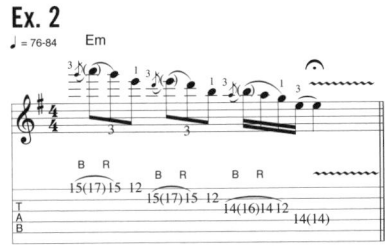

Ex. 3

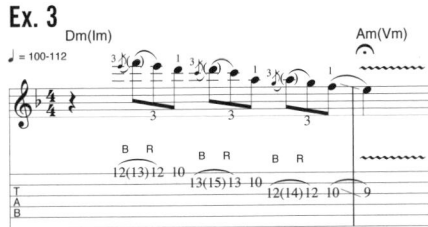

Ex. 4

Ex. 5a **Ex. 5b**

DORIAN MOVES

Next time you're playing a *G* minor blues, slip **Ex. 6** into the mix. As in the previous example, accent the first note and snap the slurs. Practice the position shift (beat two) slowly until the fingering makes sense.

In his many minor vamps, Santana often solos using the Dorian mode—one of several minor modes. Over a minor chord, you can play a Dorian line with the same root. In this example, the harmony is *Gm*, so we're in search of *G* Dorian.

Some background: The Dorian formula is 1, 2, ♭3, 4, 5, 6, ♭7. Compared to a parallel major scale, Dorian has a lowered 3 and 7. Step by step, let's work out *G* Dorian.

- Start with a *G* major scale: *G, A, B, C, D, E,* and *F♯* (1, 2, 3, 4, 5, 6, 7).
- Lowering the 3 and 7 yields *B♭* (♭3) and *F* (♭7).
- Thus *G* Dorian contains *G, A, B♭, C, D, E,* and *F* (1, 2, ♭3, 4, 5, 6, ♭7).

Ex. 6 emphasizes *E* and *B♭*—the 6 and ♭3. What's so special about these two notes? All minor modes and scales have a ♭3—it's the one note that makes them "minor." However, most minor modes and scales contain the ♭6—in this case, *E♭*—rather than the 6. By highlighting the ♭3 and 6, as in this lick, Santana accentuates the Dorian flavor.

Ex. 7, another of Santana's *G* Dorian phrases, combines the slurs from Examples 5a and 6. This two-bar figure will turn heads when you play it with conviction and a fat, squawking tone. Hit those accents in beats one, two, and three. Kenny Burrell pioneered lines like this in his blues jams with organist Jimmy Smith. Check out the soul-jazz classic *Blues Bash* (which Verve recently reissued on CD) to hear Burrell and Smith in action.

Ex. 8 features a descending *G* Dorian line on the first string. This "play along the string" technique is key to Santana's sound. In bar one, fret all the notes using your 1st finger and accent the downbeats. To play bar 2's third and fourth beats smoothly, drop a partial barre across the second and third string, simultaneously fretting *E* and *C* with your 1st finger.

OFFSET MAGIC

Santana is crafty. Unlike many rockers who stumble when soloing over major-7th chords, he knows how to make blues licks fly in jazzy settings. The secret is to offset the lick in relation to the harmony. Take **Ex. 9**, for

GUTS AND GRACE: EXPLORE THE TOUGH SENSUALITY
OF SANTANA'S LINES

Ex. 6

Ex. 7

Ex. 8

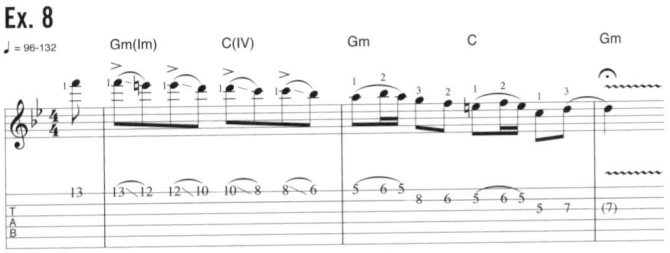

Ex. 9

instance. Melodically, this is pure Cream-era Clapton—a lick right out of "Crossroads." In that context, this would be considered an A blues phrase. But Santana uses it to connect *Cmaj7* to *Fmaj7*, and it sounds fabulous. (Be sure to hear this line against the harmony—record the changes or have someone play them. It's worth the effort, because offsetting blues licks is such an important concept.)

Here's how it works: Most blues licks contain the ♭3 and are, therefore, minor. It's the contrast of a minor melody played over a I7—say, an *A* blues lick against *A7*—that gives blues its bittersweet sound. Notice that the scale and chord roots are the same.

In this example, however, Santana plays a minor lick against its relative major chord, so the roots are offset by a minor third. The formula is easy: Play your blues lick three frets below the target major 7. When you see *Dmaj7*, play a *B* blues lick. Against *Gmaj7*, play an *E* blues lick, and so on.

Ex. 10 opens with an *A* blues lick against *Fmaj7*. This time we're riding the IVmaj7 back to the Imaj7. Just as the progression resolves to *Cmaj7*, Santana pulls out another jazz trick—the chord-over-chord technique. See how he arpeggiates an *Em* triad in those last three notes? *Em* (*E, G, B*) matches the top three chords tones in *Cmaj7* (*C, E, G, B*), so this substitution makes complete musical sense. Here's the recipe: When you see a major-7th chord, arpeggiate a minor triad starting from the major 7's 3. For *Fmaj7*, arpeggiate *Am*; for *B♭maj7*, arpeggiate *Dm*. Cool. Sustained tones play a crucial role in Santana's trademark sound, so keep that six-beat note ringing for its full value.

In **Ex. 11**, Santana reworks a country lick so it fits an *Fmaj7–Cmaj7* (IVmaj7–Imaj7) change. By itself, the figure could be a twangy honky-tonk intro in the key of *C*. Played against these major 7s, however, it sounds very smooth and uptown, proving that context is everything. Like several previous examples, this one starts on beat two.

STRING STRETCHING

The next two licks focus on Santana's bends. **Ex. 12a** is B. B. King channeled through Peter Green. Based on a series of duplicate notes on the top two strings, the line features a type of call-and-response: First, bend a whole-step to *E*; then fret *E* on the higher string. Repeat these notes to build tension that's resolved in beat four.

The quarter-bend on the and of beat four is a bit tricky: Fret both *B* and *G* with your 1st finger, hold *B* steady, and gently pull *G* toward your feet. Try this phrase with a stinging bridge-pickup tone.

GUTS AND GRACE: EXPLORE THE TOUGH SENSUALITY
OF SANTANA'S LINES

Ex. 10

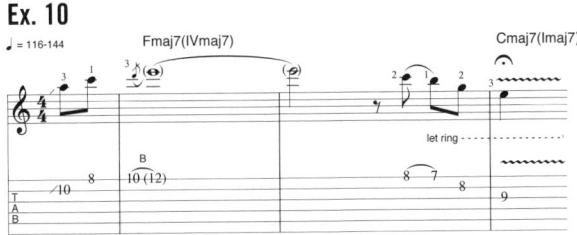

Ex. 11

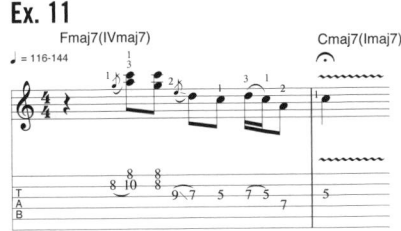

Ex. 12a
Ex. 12b

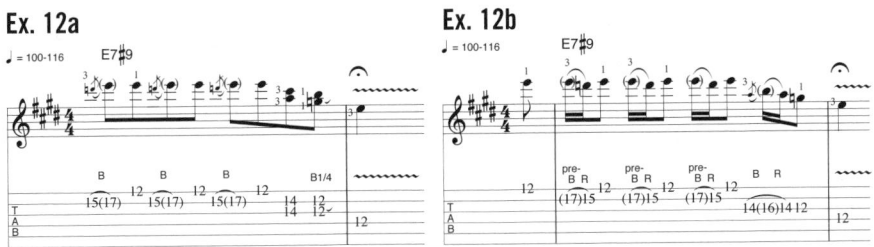

Ex. 12b is Jan Hammer channeled through Jeff Beck. Here, the game is to fret *E* on the first string, pre-bend E on the second string, and then drop down a whole-step. Again, we're using duplicate notes, but this time the fretted note precedes the bend. Ex. 12a is pure blues, Ex. 12b is certified fusion, and Santana uses them both.

Ex. 13

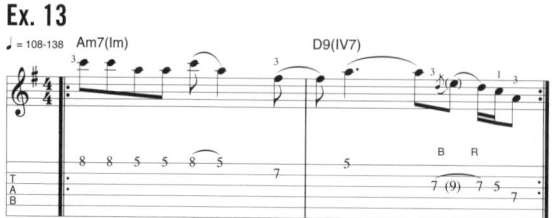

With its speech-like phrasing, **Ex. 13** is quintessential Santana. "There's cursing and praying, and all that language is part of music," he says. "A lot of my best solos remind me of when my mom used to scold me, 'Dit-doo-dup-dat-doo-doo-bah!'" Feel the rhythmic contrast between the straight eighth-notes and the following syncopations.

"Attitude is as important as notes," asserts Santana. "You learn not to be intimidated. You learn to respect and find your place—to complement. That's how I was able to survive working with John McLaughlin, because it ain't easy being with a musician like that. [*Laughs.*] When we were on the road, I thought, 'Man, what am I going to do? I should just shine his shoes.' Then I found that after he finished playing, people would go, 'Okay, we love what he says, but what do you have to say?' I may not play as many notes, or know as much as he does, but three notes—if you put them in the right place at the right time—are just as important. So when you think, 'I should hang up my guitar and be a dishwasher,' listen to your other side: 'No, you too have something they need.'"

"Don't analyze your playing. Let God light you up, and let it come out."—Carlos Santana (© JACQUES LOWE / RETNA LTD.)

13.

HOW TO PLAY LIKE CARLOS SANTANA

- -

by Jesse Gress, November 2007

Astaunch advocate of peace and universal brotherhood, Carlos Santana's guitar playing has always conveyed a similar senti-ment. Okay, maybe it's hokey to claim that you can "hear" such qualities in a guitar part, but with Carlos, well, you can actually feel the love he puts into each note.

Santana is also a devotee of the Dorian mode, and he has a particular knack for combining its characteristic sweetness with nasty blues sounds, as well as a talent for manipulating it to form other modalities. Add plenty of Latin-influenced rhythmic syncopations and a sublime, sustained tone and you've got the basic recipe for Santana stew.

Check it out: The rhythms alone in **Ex. 1** create musical excitement, but a few bluesy *D* pentatonic minor-based intervals coupled with Santana's innate sense of call-and-response add some serious sizzle.

Ex. 1

Ex. 2's run, played over a typical Im-IV progression, brings some fluttery Dorian flavor to the blues party, while **Ex. 3** reveals how Santana substitutes *F♯* Dorian (plus a few outside tones in bar 2) to create a wailing B Mixolydian modality over a ♭VII-I "A Love Supreme"-style vamp. (This last example recalls Santana's mid-'70s, Coltrane-influenced collaborations with John McLaughlin.)

Just remember that when it comes to making these tasty musical recipes successful, it's up to you to provide the main ingredient: Heart.

Ex. 2

Ex. 3

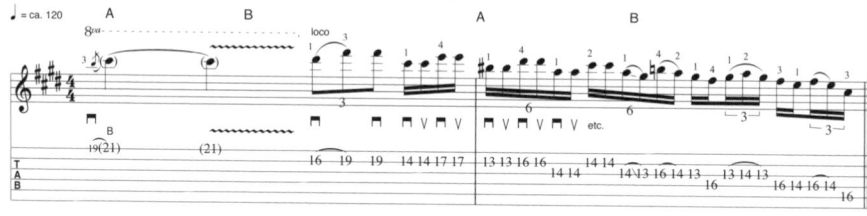

B S232   HROBW
Carlos Santana /

ROBINSON
07/11